STEPPING STONES
Through Jazz Improvisation

A Guide for Jazz Ensembles and Individuals
from Day One to the Big Gig

Bb TREBLE CLEF INSTRUMENTS

Doug Stone

Bb TREBLE CLEF INSTRUMENTS

Published by Low Down Publishing

ISBN-13: 978-1-7353277-9-2

Editing: John Mills
Cover Design: Alison Coté
Interior Layout: Lauren Woodrow
Notation Engraving: Marc Schwartz

Foreword by
Jamey Aebersold

For more about the author, visit:
www.dougstonejazz.com

Acknowledgements

I would like to thank Danny Ziemann for his friendship, encouragement, vision, and faith in what I do. The way Danny supports his colleagues on the bandstand with solid, musical, swinging quarter-note bass lines is reminiscent of the way he supports his friends in life with strength, articulated thoughts, and consistent contact. Without Danny I would have continued sharing my ideas with a few students at a time in small band rooms here and there, but I never would have shared them with the world through this book.

Table of Contents

Foreword

Doug Stone was 12 years old when I met him and his father at the Illinois Music Educators convention in Peoria, Illinois. Doug was playing alto sax and was excited to meet me. We had lunch together and not long after, his father sent me a VHS video tape of Doug playing with my Volume 24, Major and Minor Play-A-Long. He was going up and down the scales like a pro and I knew this kid was serious.

It gives me great pleasure to endorse this new contribution to the plethora of jazz educational books.

Doug is a master player and has paid attention to the process of using the basics, scales and chords along with rhythms, articulations and bits and pieces of the jazz language to help students carve their way through the early stages of learning to play jazz. Keep in mind that jazz solos are based on what each individual person is hearing in their mind while playing their solo. Doug's book helps clear up misconceptions about playing jazz and improvising. You don't JUST PLAY until you know what to play.

This book will be a staple for years to come. It's practical, understandable, usable and FUN. Since all music is based on scales and chords, learning them in different keys is essential when mastering one's instrument. Doug has paid attention to the formative needs of the beginning and intermediate improvisor. This book provides the needed harmonic material for soloing on various songs and I personally would have made more progress as a teenager if this book had been suggested to me by my music teachers.

Band directors and private instructors can use this with their students at any stage of development. This book coupled with the teacher's imagination will give the student a well-rounded approach to playing jazz and a strong foundation for applying jazz theory.

Now, long after first hearing Doug, he has become a world-class player and will make a lasting impact on jazz education with **Stepping Stones Through Jazz Improvisation**.

Congratulations to Doug for taking the time and energy to put his thoughts and experience into something that will outlast him.

—Jamey Aebersold

Introduction

"Anyone can improvise."
—Jamey Abersold, National Endowment for the Arts Jazz Master

I believe this with all my heart. I have heard students of all ages and experience levels play rhythmically meaningful, melodically engaging, harmonically accurate, and historically rooted jazz improvisations. I have also heard students and teachers express fear about learning and teaching jazz improvisation. This book presents a straightforward, detailed, and sequential approach to the study of jazz improvisation. It can be used by individuals or in ensemble contexts, regardless of instrument or voice type.

I hope to encourage students and teachers to avoid the "just play this scale and you will sound fine" approach to jazz improvisation. When jazz musicians improvise they are typically following a harmonic format. Making bluesy melodies with a minor pentatonic or blues scale is a great tool and an important aspect of jazz improvisation, but that approach alone can lead to musical misunderstanding.

Improvising using only the roots of the chords, played at the proper time, creates a foundation for meaningful and accurate jazz improvisation. The root, scale, and arpeggio exercises in this book are meant to create a technical foundation to prevent students from building their musical language "on top of confusion and vagueness," to quote legendary jazz pianist Bill Evans.

After building a solid harmonic foundation through root, scale, and arpeggio exercises, this book introduces "riffs" (simple, bluesy, melodies that can be linked to decades of improvised jazz and blues solos). When improvising with riffs, it is imperative to organize the solo in relationship to the harmonic form. Improvisers can use one riff for an entire chorus, create an AAB riff scheme, or use different riffs every two or four measures, but they must relate their solos to the form. Riffs need to be played with appropriate style and articulation.

Articulations are provided throughout the book to help, but, I also highly recommend a thorough study of "doodle-tonguing." For detailed information on correct jazz articulation, please review Ronald Carter's chapter in **Teaching Music through Performance in Jazz** entitled "A Multi-Cultural Approach to Jazz Education."

Jazz ensemble directors can utilize this book to

1. teach students improvisation, and
2. create a complete arrangement replete with
   a. introduction.
   b. melody based on riffs.
   c. solos that include root, scale, and arpeggio elements.
   d. riff solos.
   e. backgrounds using scale notes and riffs.
   f. shout chorus.

All the while, directors will be teaching students harmonic and formal elements, jazz language, articulation, style, and feel.

This curriculum has been tried and tested. I have personally taught these concepts to young and inexperienced students, adult amateurs, advanced high school students, college jazz majors, and even professional big bands. This material originated from professional opportunities that required me to teach jazz improvisation in order to get paid! But, it has evolved into a method that teaches correct musical principles that can change students' lives. If you trust this process, you will believe as I do that "anyone can improvise" jazz.

—Doug Stone

B ♭ BLUES PRACTICE PROCEDURE

swing at 120 BPM

Roots

1a. Roots

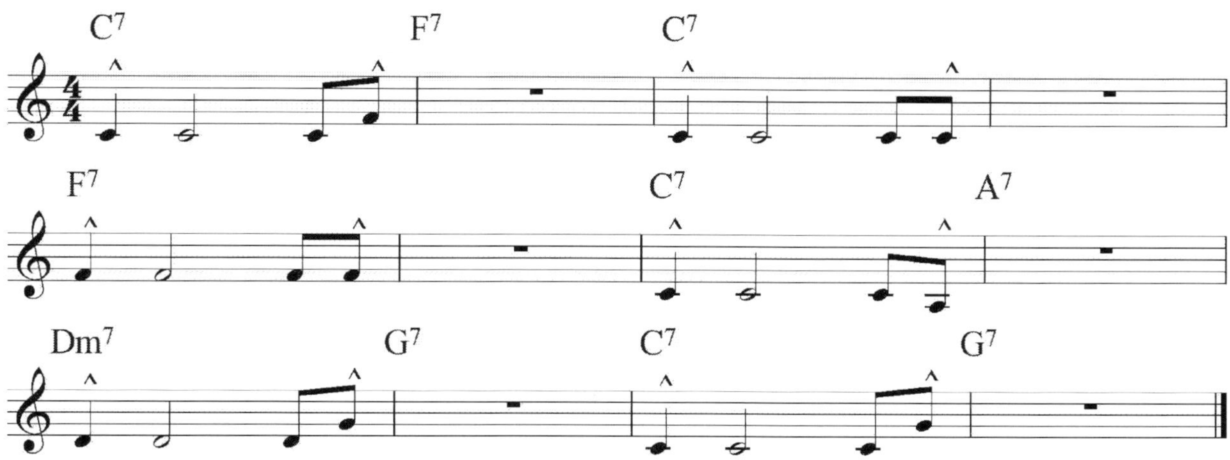

Play an improvised solo using only the roots of the chord.

1b. Roots — sample improvised solo

1c. Roots — play an improvised solo using only roots

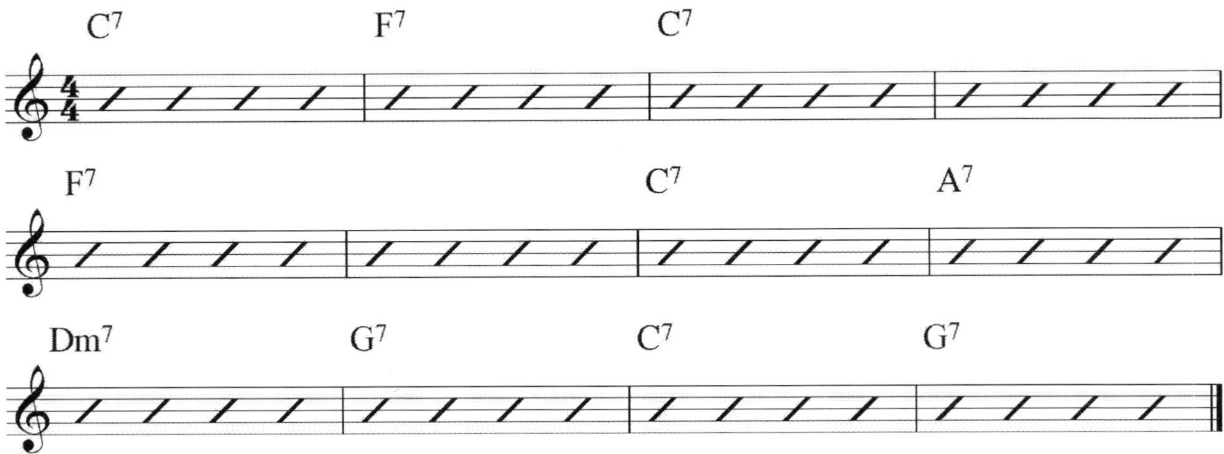

1, 2, 3's

2a. 1, 2, 3's — up up

2b. 1, 2, 3's — up down

2c. 1, 2, 3's — down up

2d. 1, 2, 3's — down down

Play an improvised solo using only 1, 2, 3's of each scale.

2e. 1, 2, 3's — sample improvised solo

2f. 1, 2, 3's — play an improvised solo using only 1, 2, 3's

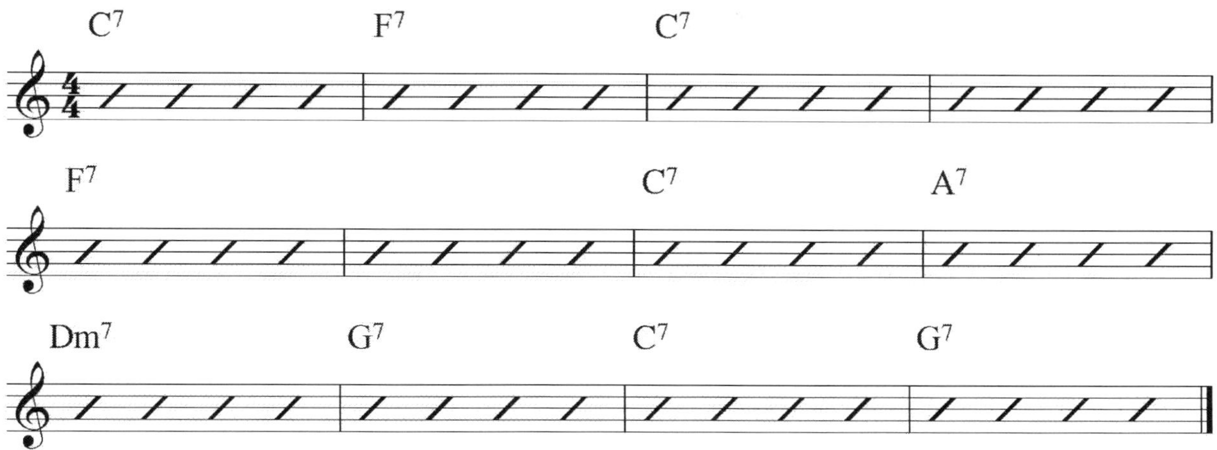

1, 2, 3, 4, 5's

3a. 1, 2, 3, 4, 5's — up up

3b. 1, 2, 3, 4, 5's — up down

3c. 1, 2, 3, 4, 5's — down up

3d. 1, 2, 3, 4, 5's — down down

Play an improvised solo using only 1, 2, 3, 4, 5's of each scale.

3e. 1, 2, 3, 4, 5's — sample improvised solo

3f. 1, 2, 3, 4, 5's — play an improvised solo using only 1, 2, 3, 4, 5's

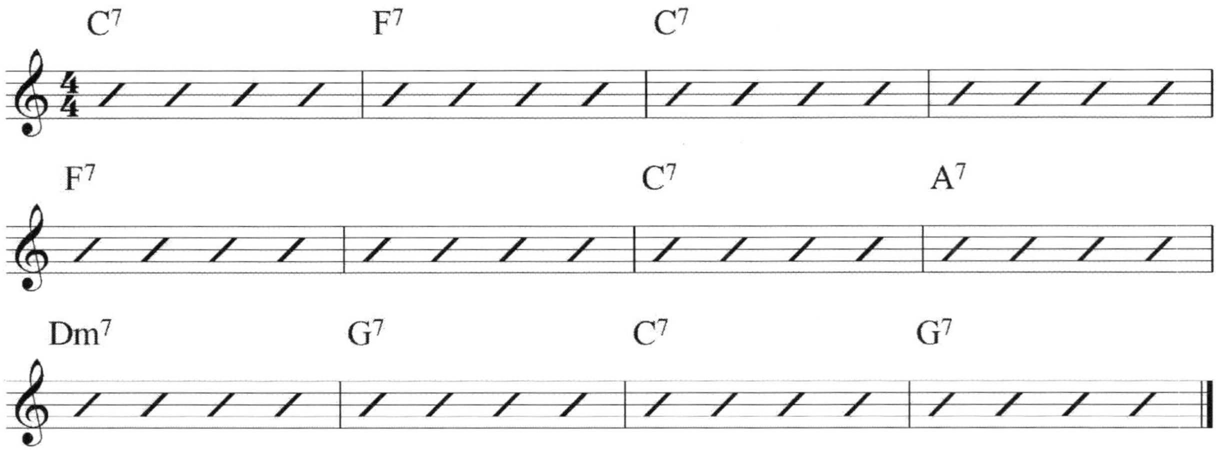

Full Scales

During perpetual motion exercises, stop to breathe, but keep your fingers, keys, and slides moving while breathing.

4a. Full scales — up up

4b. Full scales — up down

4c. Full scales — down up

4d. Full scales — down down

Play an improvised solo using any scale notes.

4e. Full scales — sample improvised solo

4f. Full Scales — play an improvised solo using any scale notes

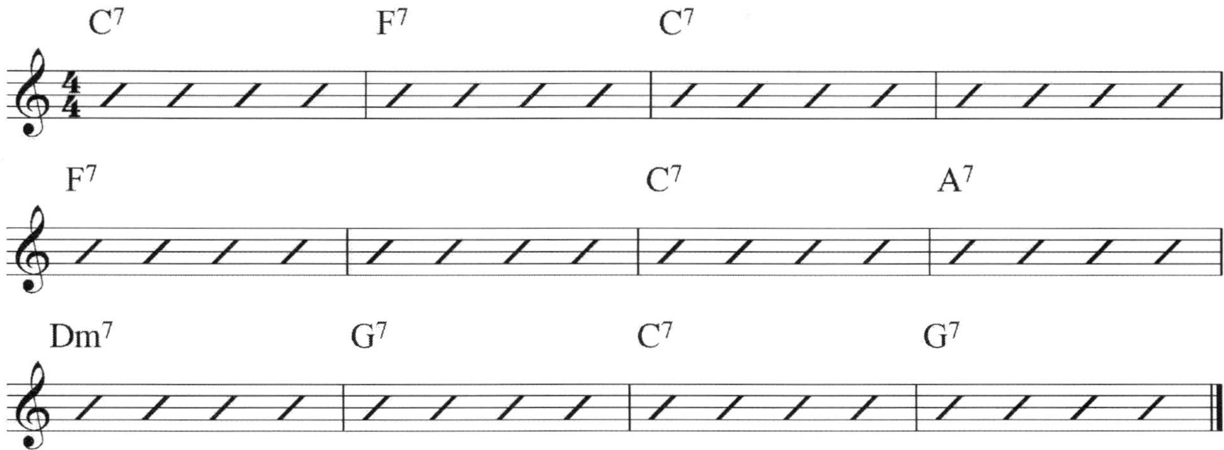

Chord Tone Workout

5a. 1, 3, 5, 7 — up up

5b. 1, 3, 5, 7 — up down

5c. 1, 3, 5, 7 — down up

5d. 1, 3, 5, 7 — down down

6a. 3, 5, 7, 1 — up up

6b. 3, 5, 7, 1 — up down

6c. 3, 5, 7, 1 — down up

6d. 3, 5, 7, 1 — down down

7a. 5, 7, 1, 3 — up up

7b. 5, 7, 1, 3 — up down

7c. 5, 7, 1, 3 — down up

7d. 5, 7, 1, 3 — down down

8a. 7, 1, 3, 5 — up up

8b. 7, 1, 3, 5 — up down

8c. 7, 1, 3, 5 — down up

8d. 7, 1, 3, 5 — down down

9. Bebop / ii-V Vocab — an introduction to bebop chromaticism

10. Running eighth-notes with chord tones on down beats

B ♭ to B ♭ (two octaves) — chromaticism used to connect when necessary

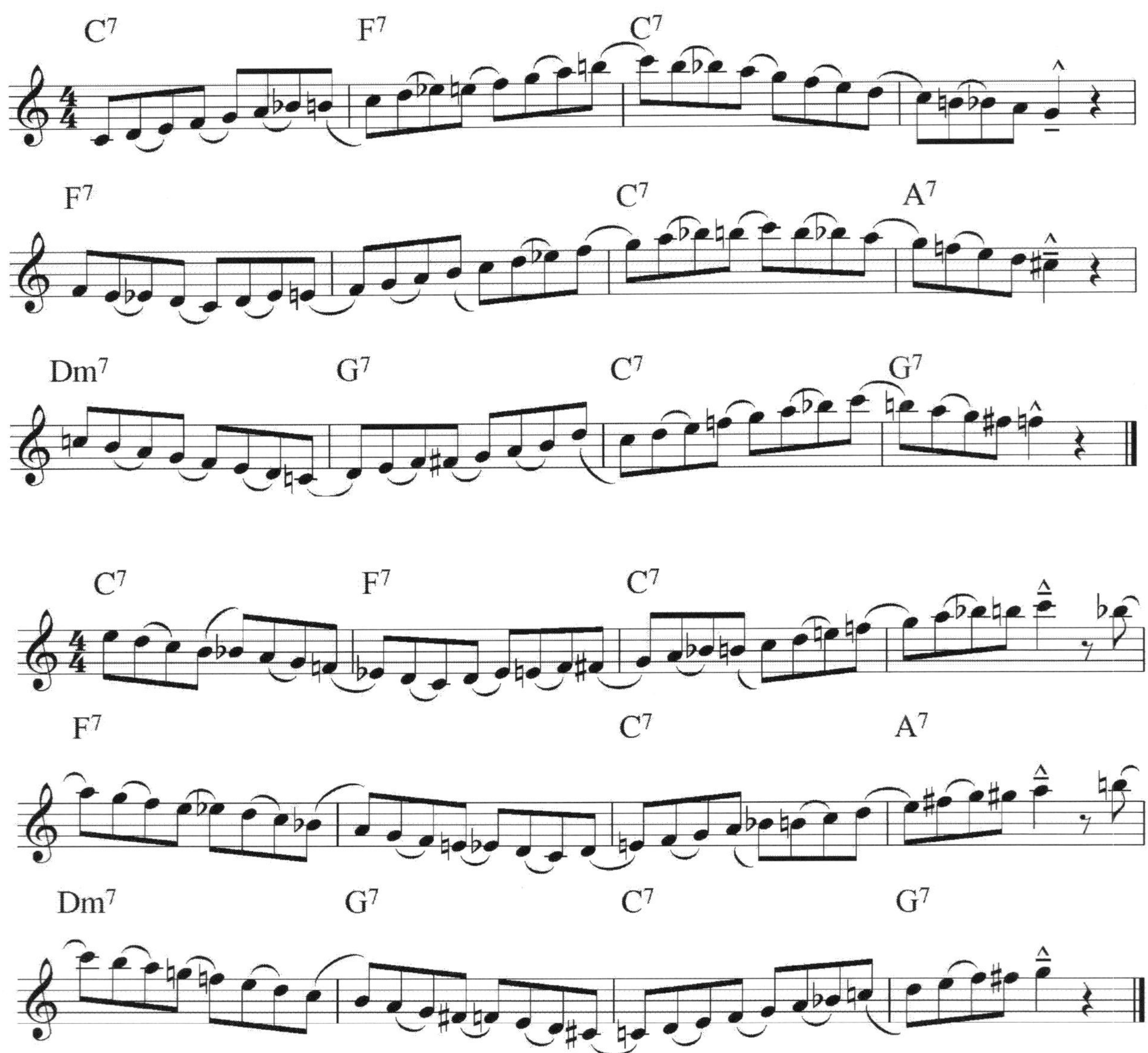

Minor Pentatonic Riffs

"Call" #1

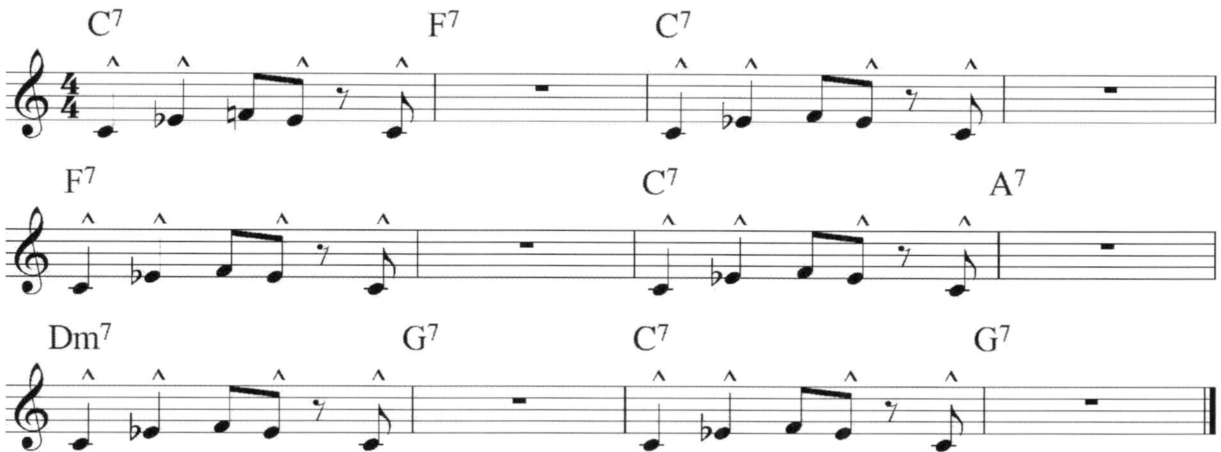

"Response" #1

"Longer Riff" #1

"Call" #2

"Response" #2

"Longer Riff" #2

"Call" #3

"Response" #3

"Longer Riff" #3

"Call" #4

"Response" #4

"Longer Riff" #4

"Call" #5

"Response" #5

"Longer Riff" #5

4 Sample Improvised Choruses using Minor Pentatonic Riffs

Chorus #1

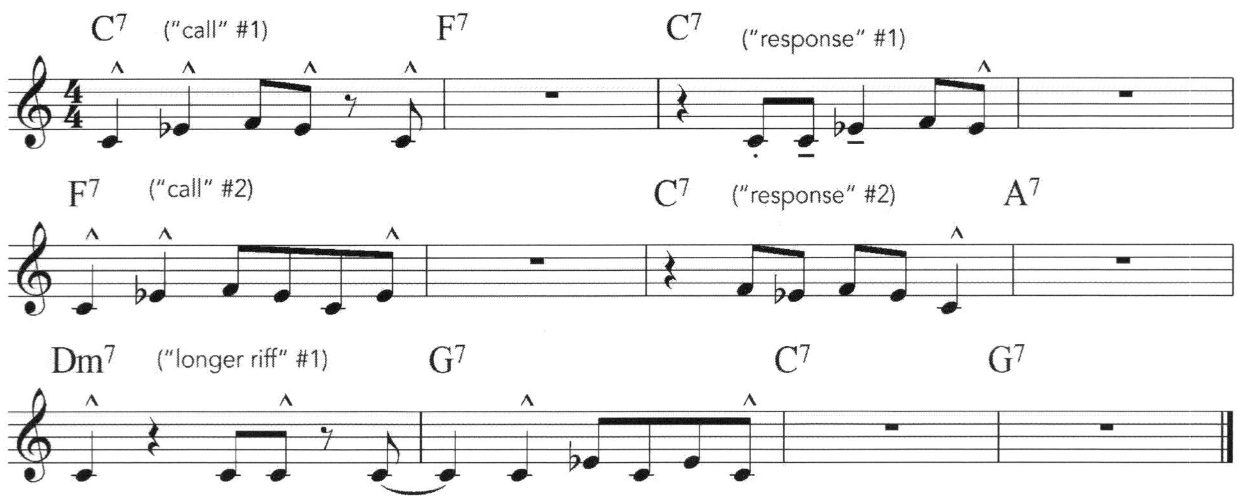

Chorus #2

Chorus #3 — AAB phrases

Chorus #4 — AAB phrases

Play an improvised solo using minor pentatonic riffs.

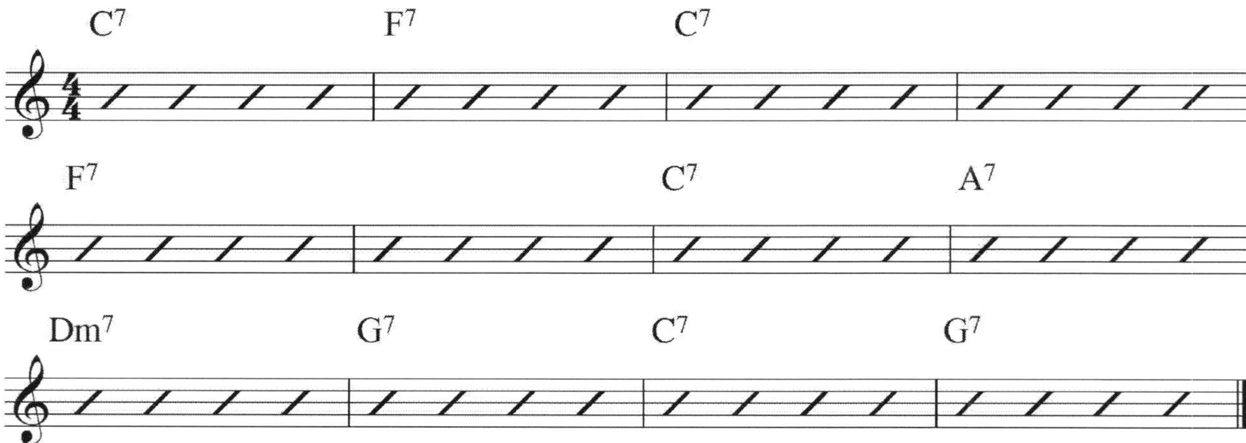

C MINOR BLUES PRACTICE PROCEDURE

swing at 105 BPM

Roots

1a. Roots

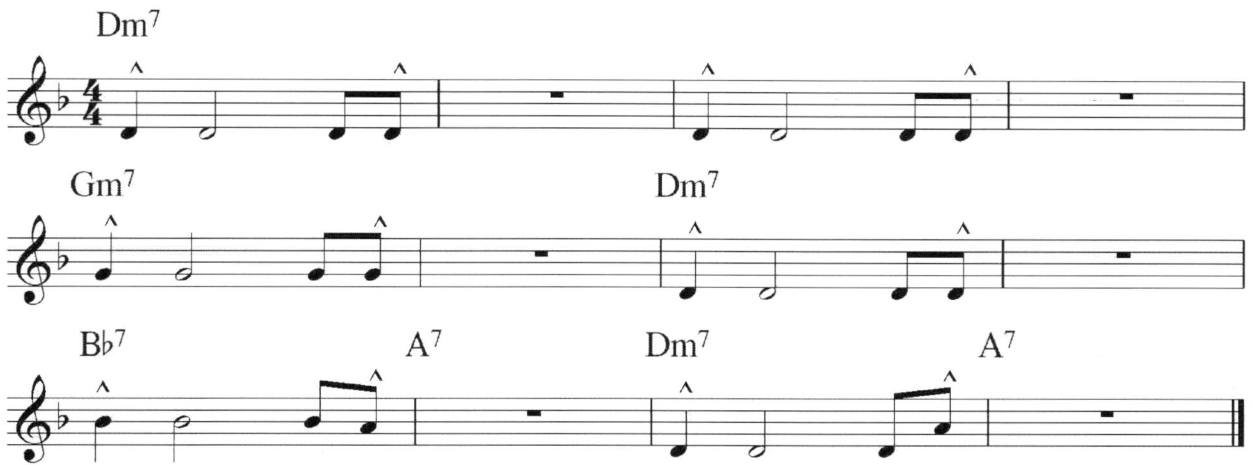

Play an improvised solo using only the roots of the chord.

1b. Roots — sample improvised solo

1c. Roots — play an improvised solo using only roots

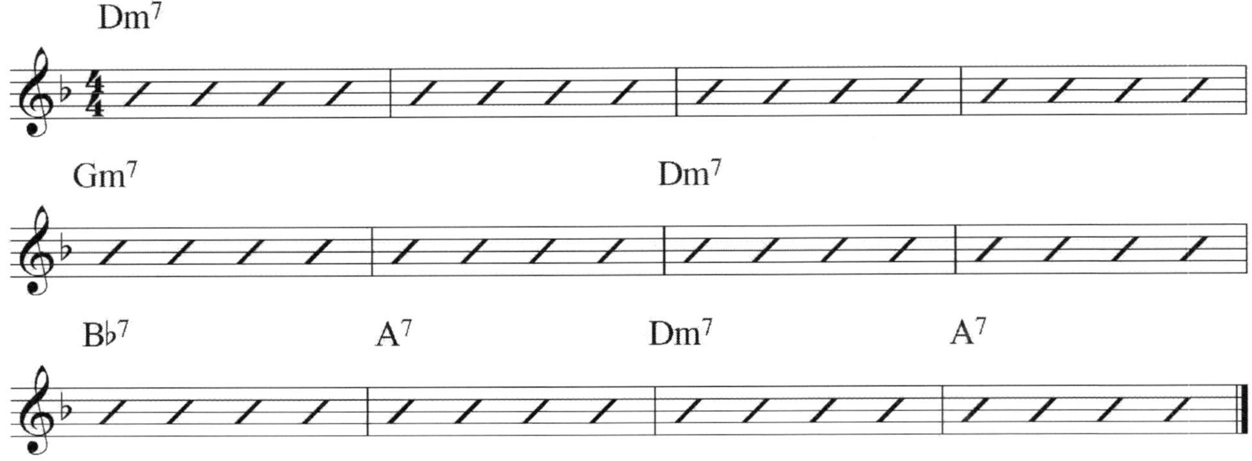

1, 2, 3's

2a. 1, 2, 3's — up up

2b. 1, 2, 3's — up down

2c. 1, 2, 3's — down up

2d. 1, 2, 3's — down down

Play an improvised solo using only 1, 2, 3's of each scale.

2e. 1, 2, 3's — sample improvised solo

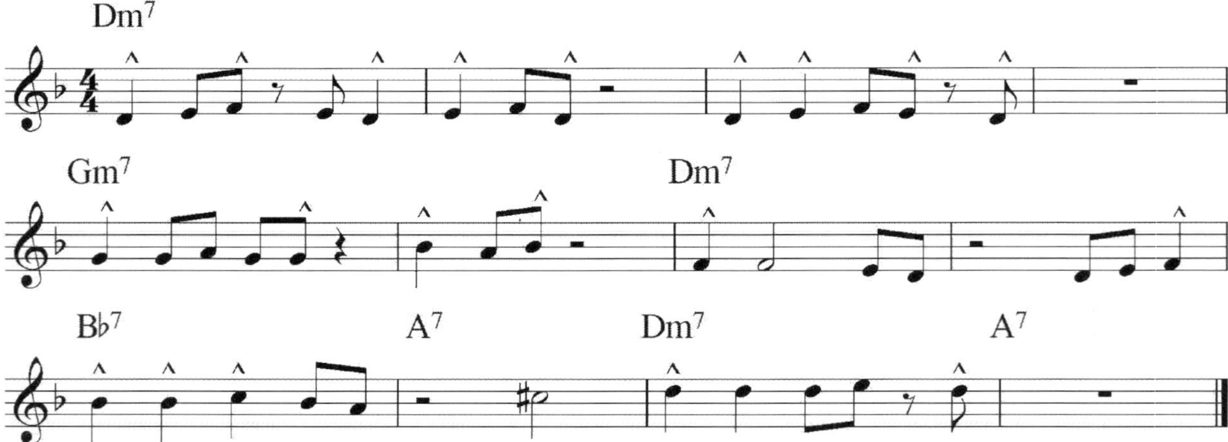

2f. 1, 2, 3's — play an improvised solo using only 1, 2, 3's

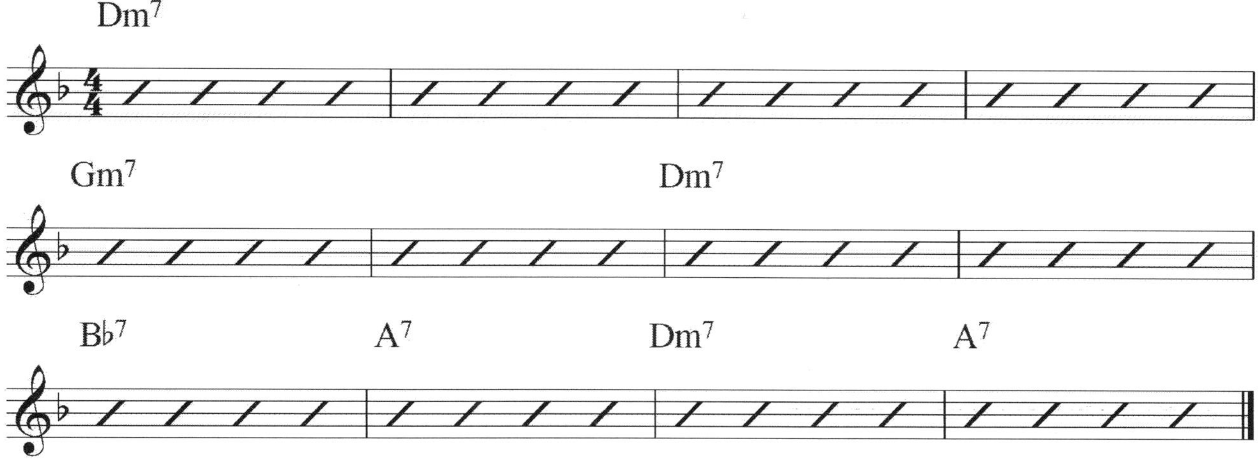

1, 2, 3, 4, 5's

3a. 1, 2, 3, 4, 5's — up up

3b. 1, 2, 3, 4, 5's — up down

3c. 1, 2, 3, 4, 5's — down up

3d. 1, 2, 3, 4, 5's — down down

Play an improvised solo using only 1, 2, 3, 4, 5's of each scale.

3e. 1, 2, 3, 4, 5's — sample improvised solo

3f. 1, 2, 3, 4, 5's — play an improvised solo using only 1, 2, 3, 4, 5's

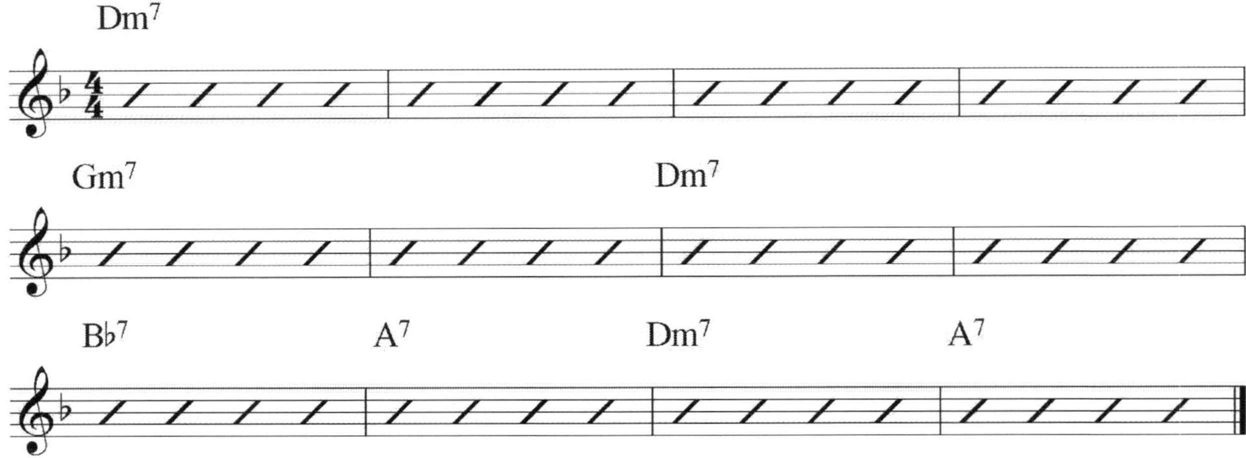

Full Scales

During perpetual motion exercises, stop to breathe, but keep your fingers, keys, and slides moving while breathing.

4a. Full scales — up up

4b. Full scales — up down

4c. Full scales — down up

4d. Full scales — down down

Play an improvised solo using any scale notes.

4e. Full scales — sample improvised solo

4f. Full Scales — play an improvised solo using any scale notes

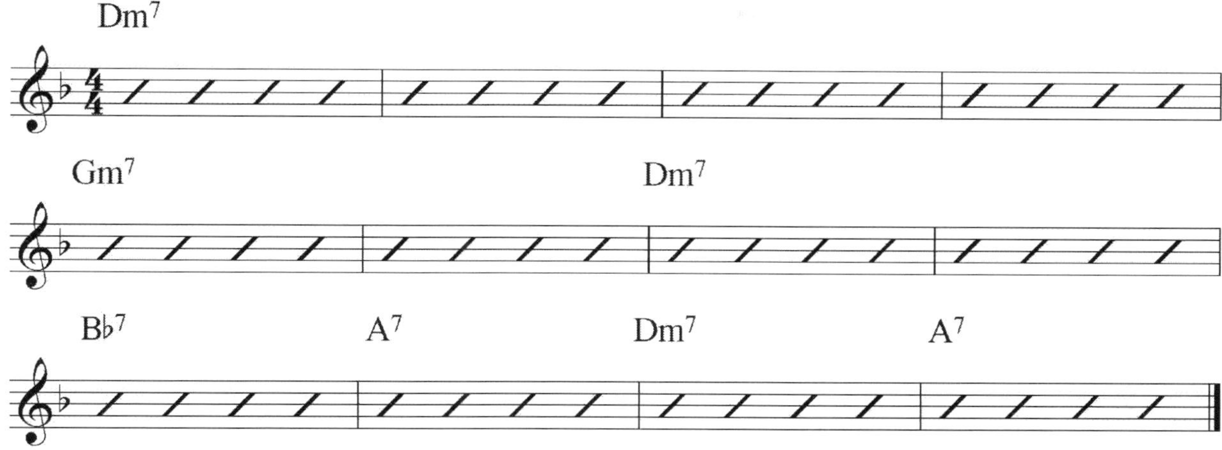

Chord Tone Workout

5a. 1, 3, 5, 7 — up up

5b. 1, 3, 5, 7 — up down

5c. 1, 3, 5, 7 — down up

5d. 1, 3, 5, 7 — down down

6a. 3, 5, 7, 1 — up up

6b. 3, 5, 7, 1 — up down

6c. 3, 5, 7, 1 — down up

6d. 3, 5, 7, 1 — down down

7a. 5, 7, 1, 3 — up up

7b. 5, 7, 1, 3 — up down

7c. 5, 7, 1, 3 — down up

7d. 5, 7, 1, 3 — down down

8a. 7, 1, 3, 5 — up up

8b. 7, 1, 3, 5 — up down

8c. 7, 1, 3, 5 — down up

8d. 7, 1, 3, 5 — down down

9. Minor Blues Vocab

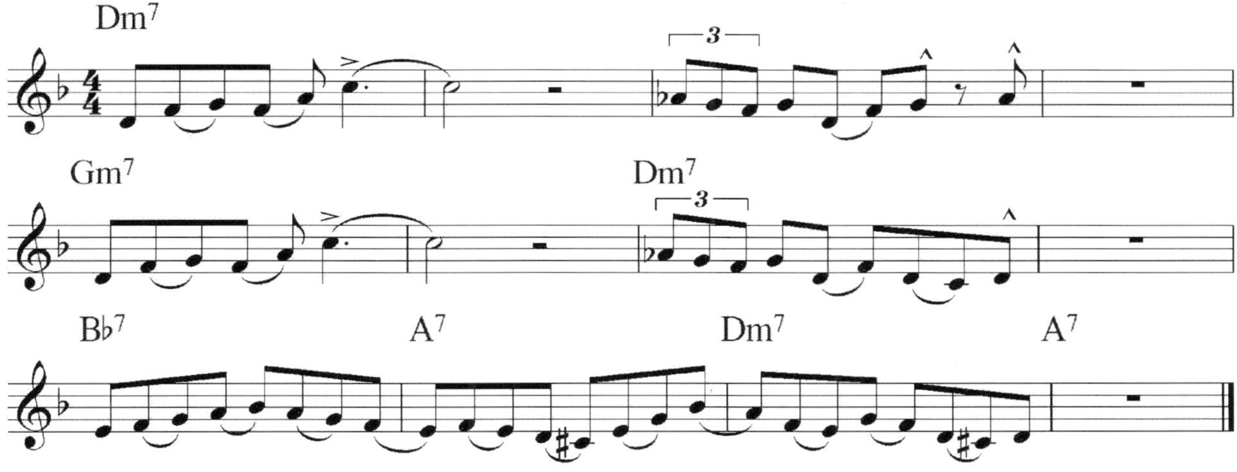

10. Running eighth-notes with chord tones on down beats

C to C (two octaves) — chromaticism used to connect when necessary

Minor Pentatonic Riffs

"Call" #1

"Response" #1

"Longer Riff" #1

"Call" #2

"Response" #2

"Longer Riff" #2

"Call" #3

"Response" #3

"Longer Riff" #3

"Call" #4

"Response" #4

"Longer Riff" #4

"Call" #5

"Response" #5

"Longer Riff" #5

4 Sample Improvised Choruses using Minor Pentatonic Riffs

Chorus #1

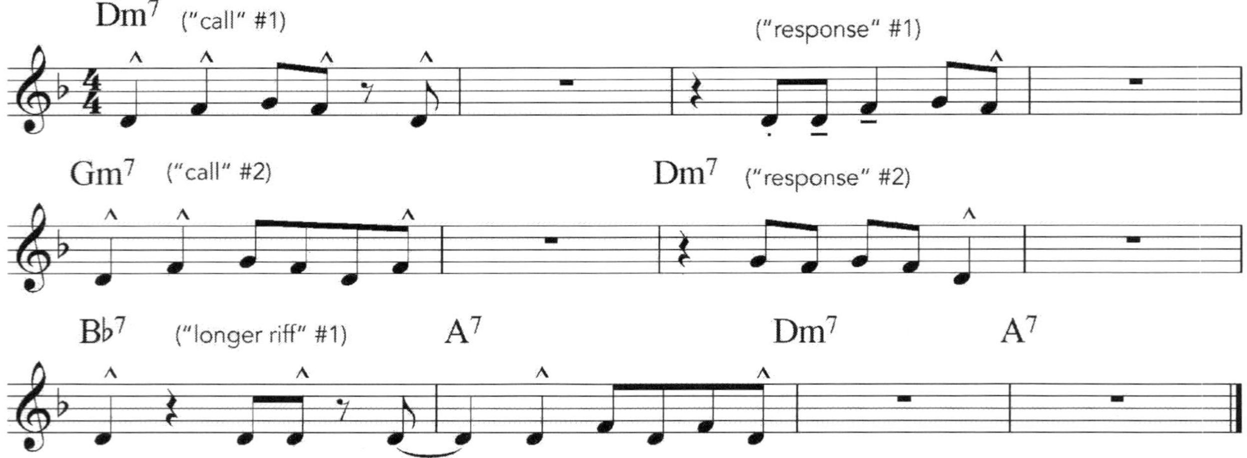

Chorus #2

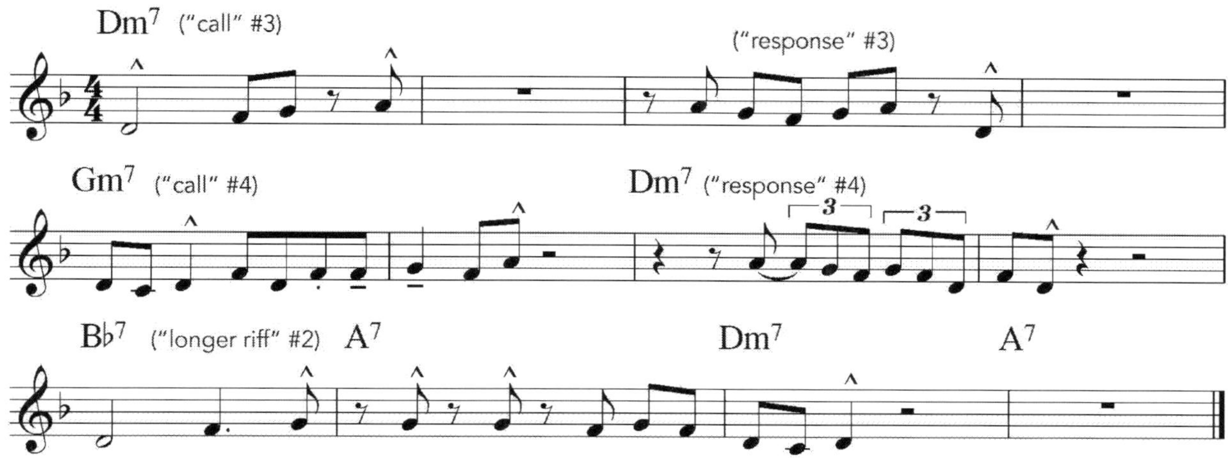

Chorus #3 — AAB phrases

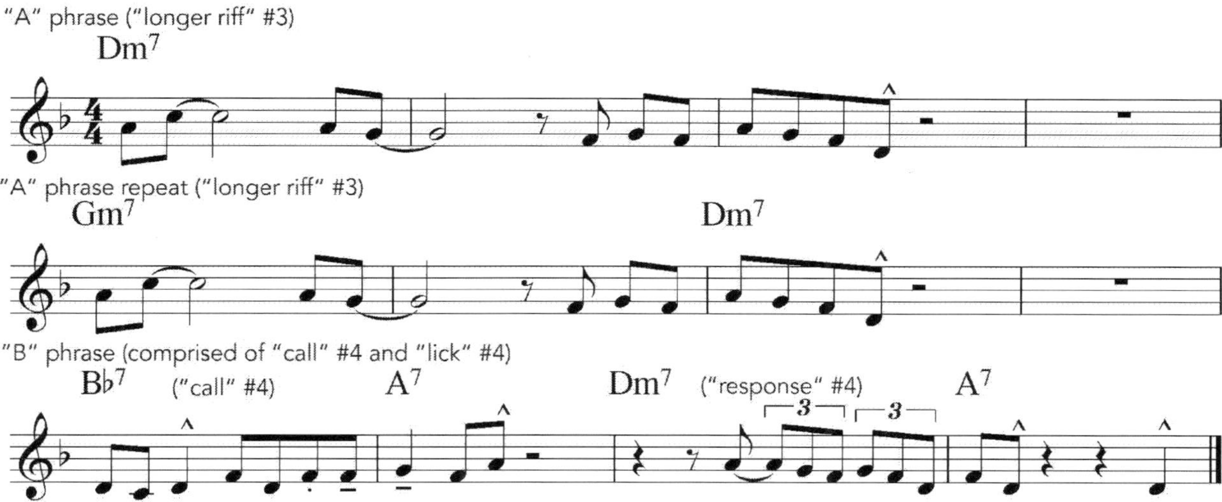

Chorus #4 — AAB phrases

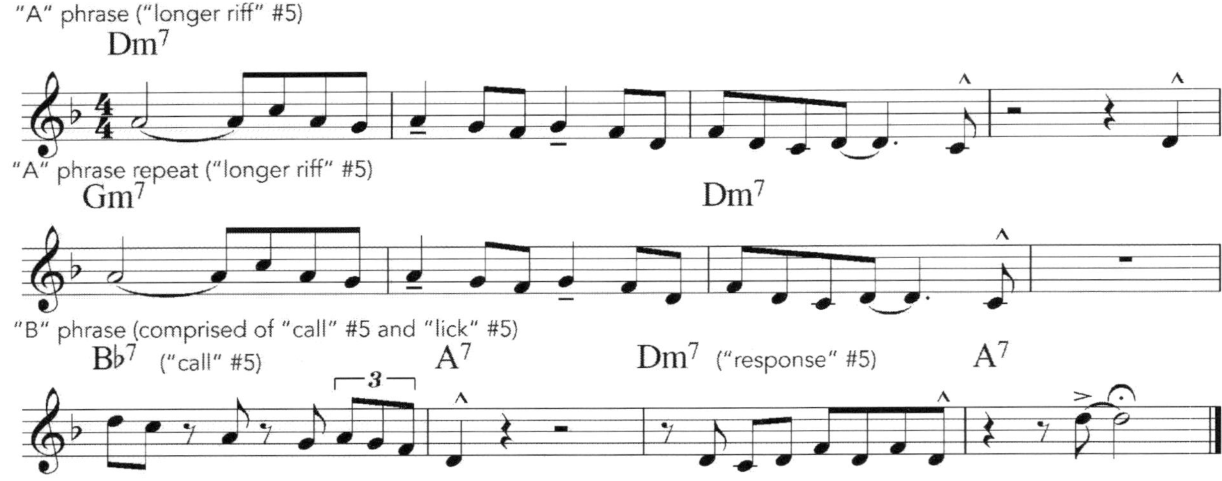

Play an improvised solo using minor pentatonic riffs.

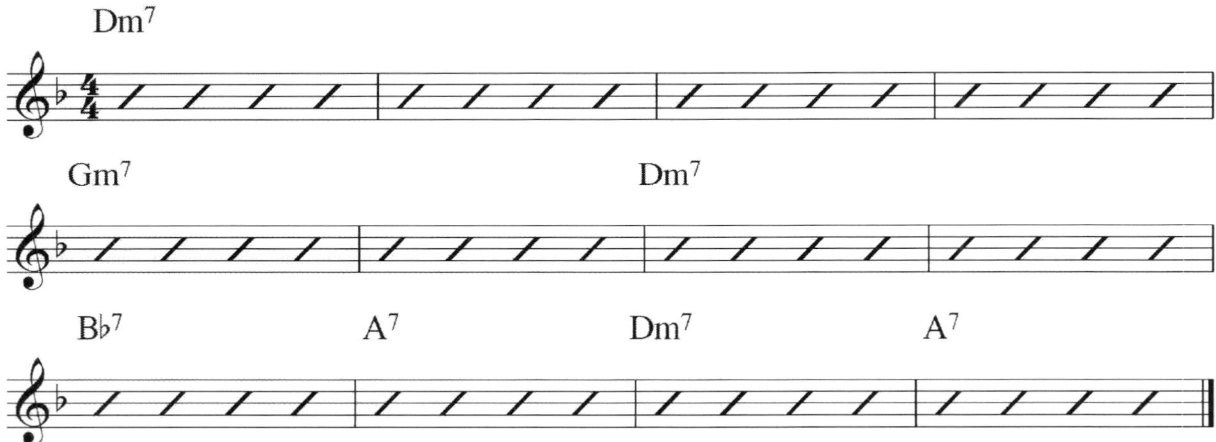

G MINOR BLUES PRACTICE PROCEDURE

swing at 105 BPM

Roots

1a. Roots

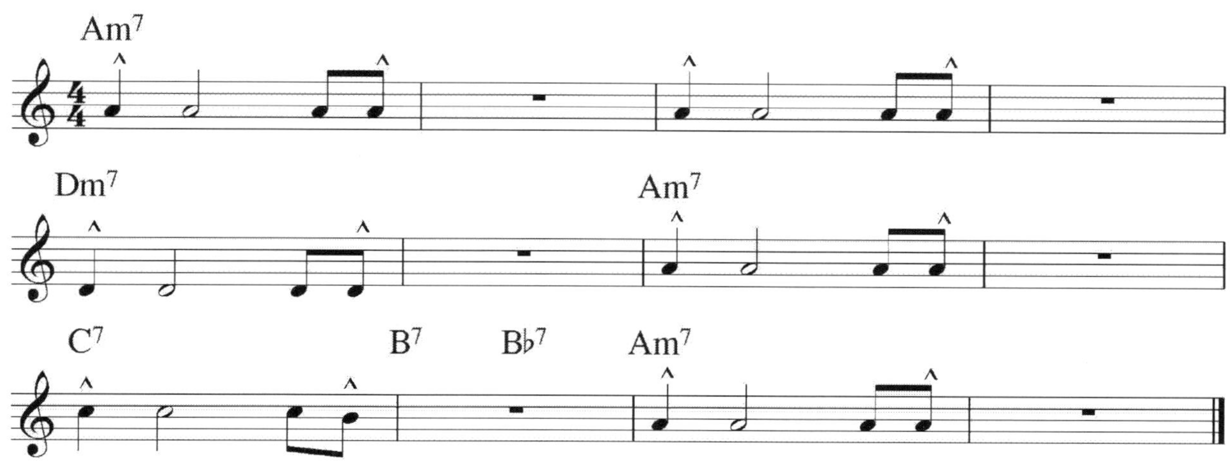

Play an improvised solo using only the roots of the chord.

1b. Roots — sample improvised solo

1c. Roots — play an improvised solo using only roots

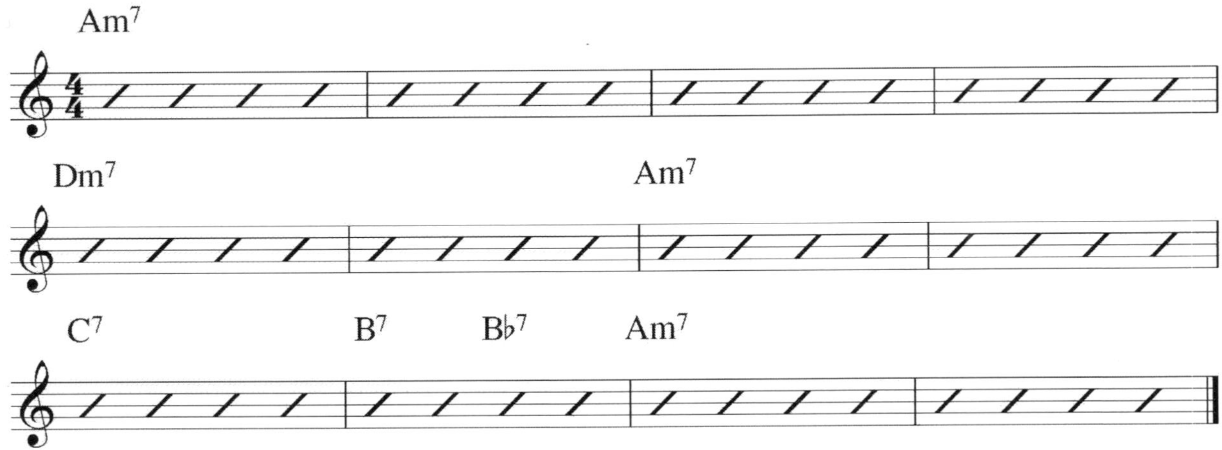

1, 2, 3's

2a. 1, 2, 3's — up up

2b. 1, 2, 3's — up down

2c. 1, 2, 3's — down up

2d. 1, 2, 3's — down down

Play an improvised solo using only 1, 2, 3's of each scale.

2e. 1, 2, 3's — sample improvised solo

2f. 1, 2, 3's — play an improvised solo using only 1, 2, 3's

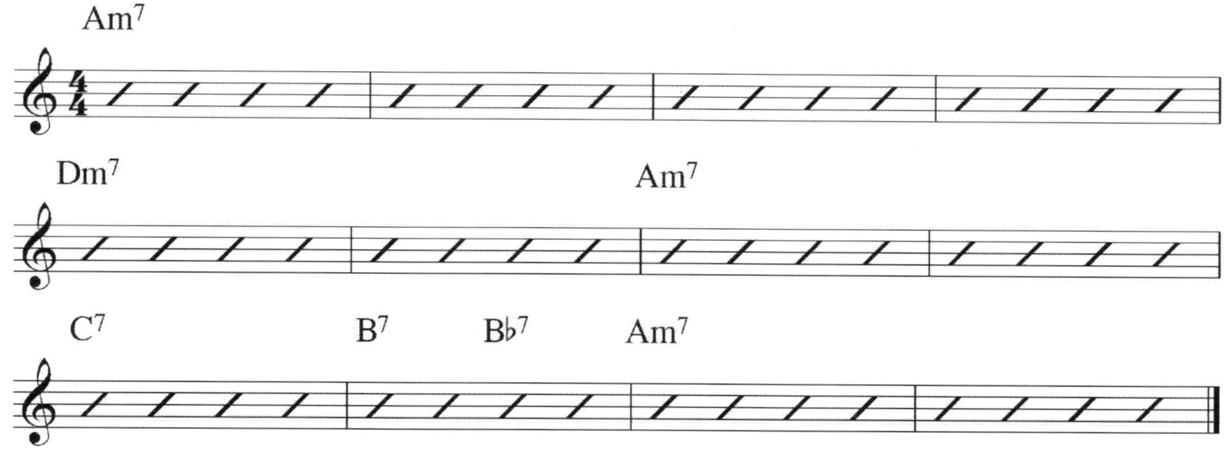

1, 2, 3, 4, 5's

3a. 1, 2, 3, 4, 5's — up up

3b. 1, 2, 3, 4, 5's — up down

3c. 1, 2, 3, 4, 5's — down up

3d. 1, 2, 3, 4, 5's — down down

Play an improvised solo using only 1, 2, 3, 4, 5's of each scale.

3e. 1, 2, 3, 4, 5's — sample improvised solo

3f. 1, 2, 3, 4, 5's — play an improvised solo using only 1, 2, 3, 4, 5's

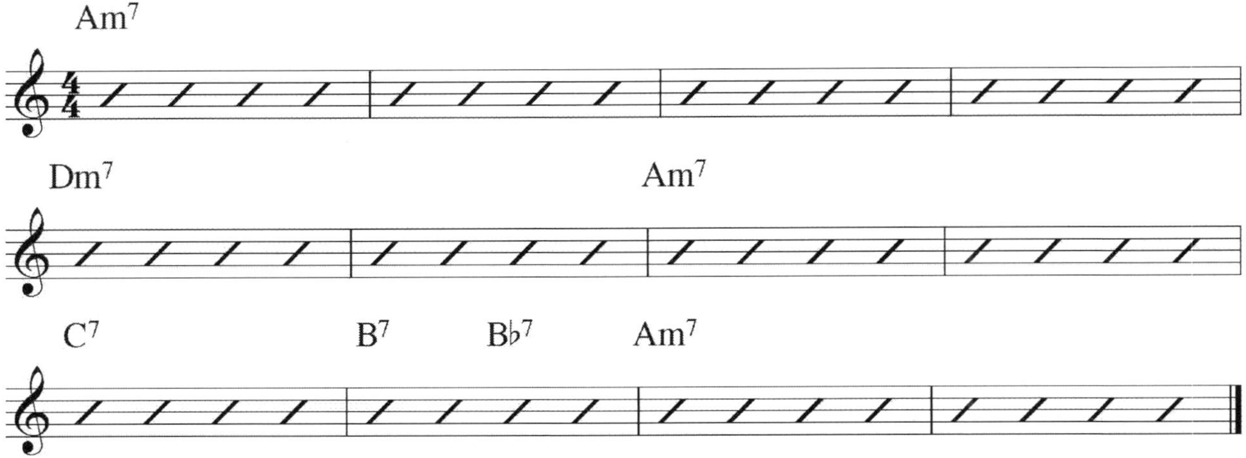

Full Scales

During perpetual motion exercises, stop to breathe, but keep your fingers, keys, and slides moving while breathing.

4a. Full scales — up up

4b. Full scales — up down

4c. Full scales — down up

4d. Full scales — down down

Play an improvised solo using any scale notes.

4e. Full scales — sample improvised solo

Chord Tone Workout

5a. 1, 3, 5, 7 — up up

5b. 1, 3, 5, 7 — up down

5c. 1, 3, 5, 7 — down up

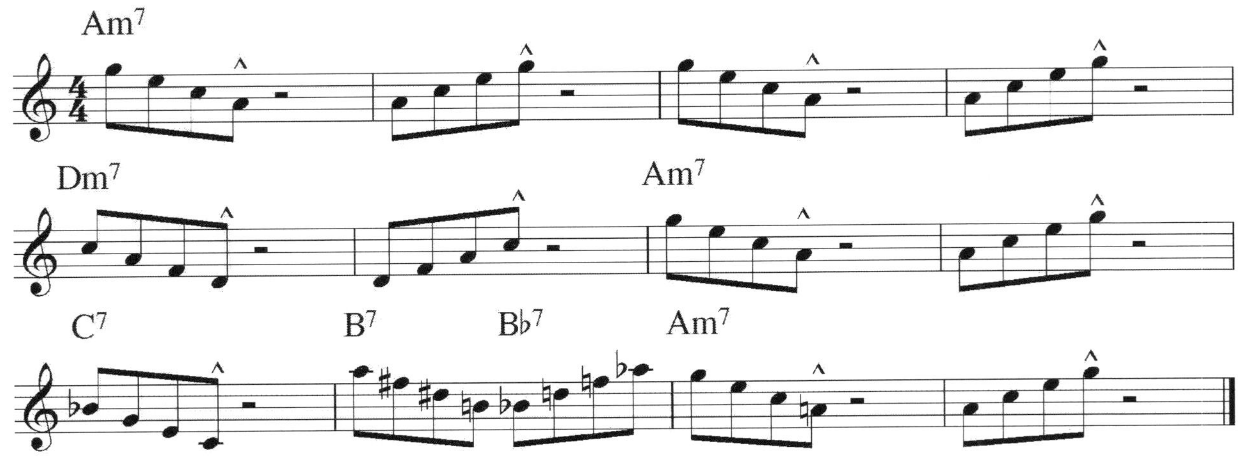

5d. 1, 3, 5, 7 — down down

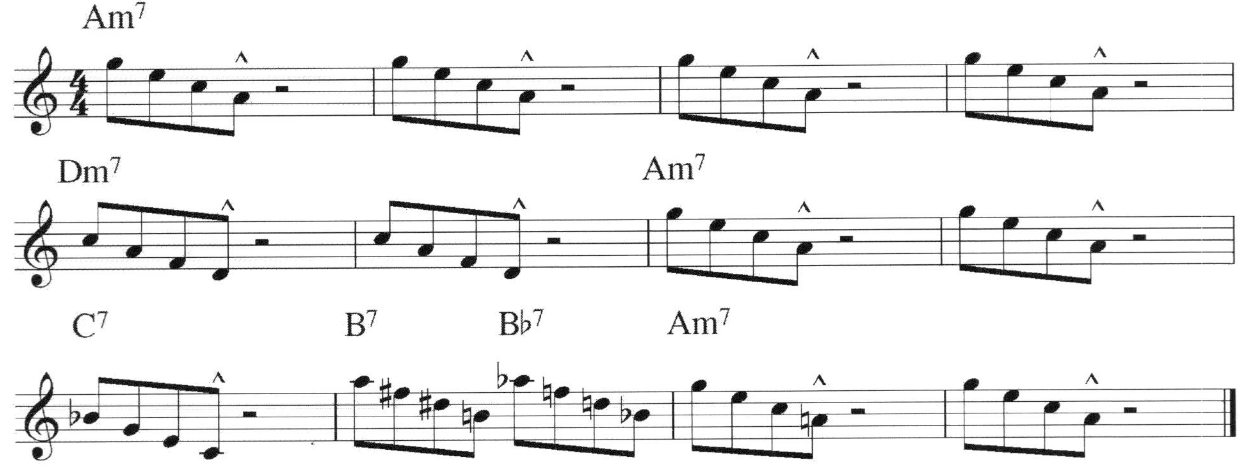

6a. 3, 5, 7, 1 — up up

6b. 3, 5, 7, 1 — up down

6c. 3, 5, 7, 1 — down up

6d. 3, 5, 7, 1 — down down

7a. 5, 7, 1, 3 — up up

7b. 5, 7, 1, 3 — up down

7c. 5, 7, 1, 3 — down up

7d. 5, 7, 1, 3 — down down

8a. 7, 1, 3, 5 — up up

8b. 7, 1, 3, 5 — up down

8c. 7, 1, 3, 5 — down up

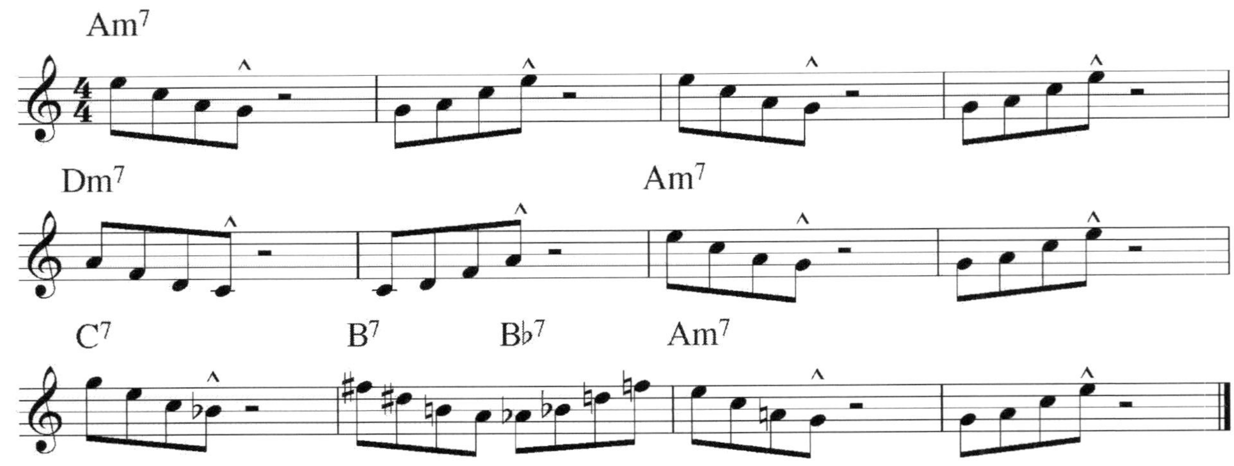

8d. 7, 1, 3, 5 — down down

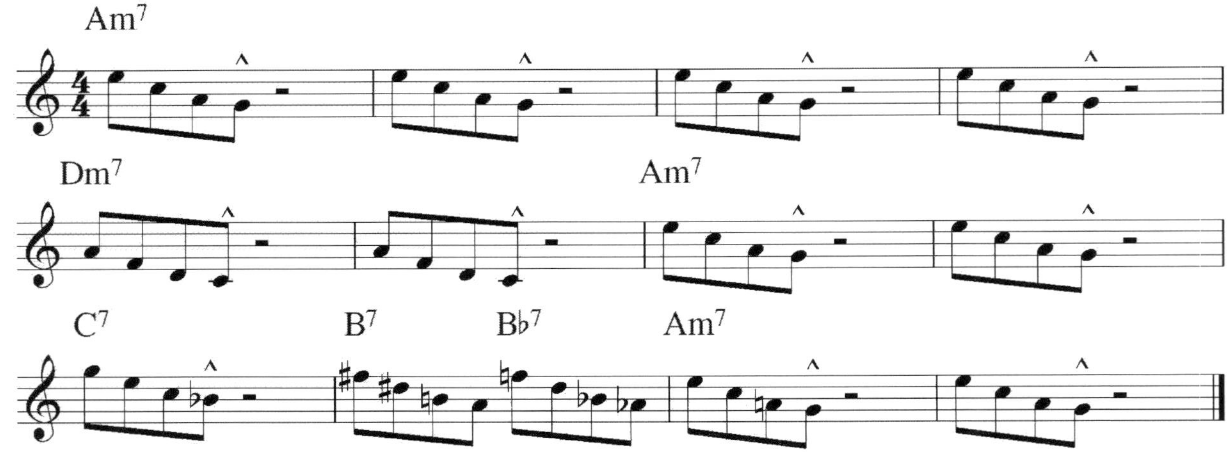

9. Minor Blues Vocab

Am7
Dm7
Am7
C7
B7
Bb7
Am7

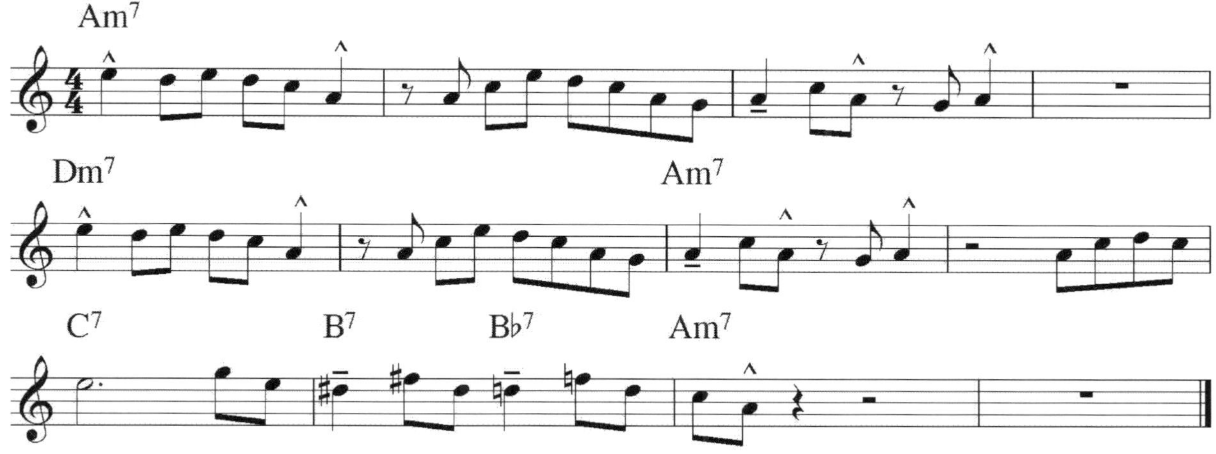

10. Running eighth-notes with chord tones on down beats

G to G (two octaves) — chromaticism used to connect when necessary

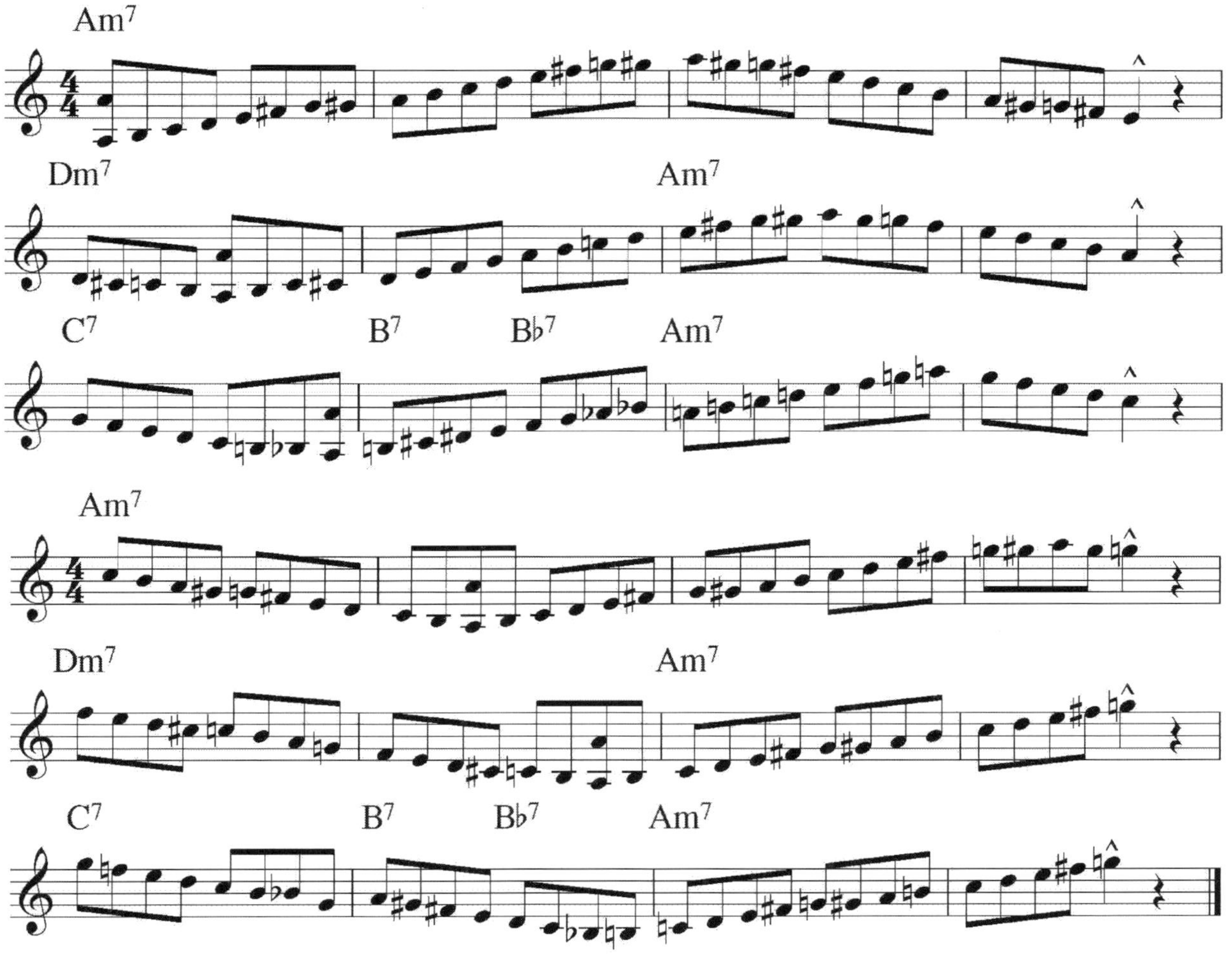
Am7
Dm7
Am7
C7
B7
Bb7
Am7
Am7
Dm7
Am7
C7
B7
Bb7
Am7

Minor Pentatonic Riffs

"Call" #1

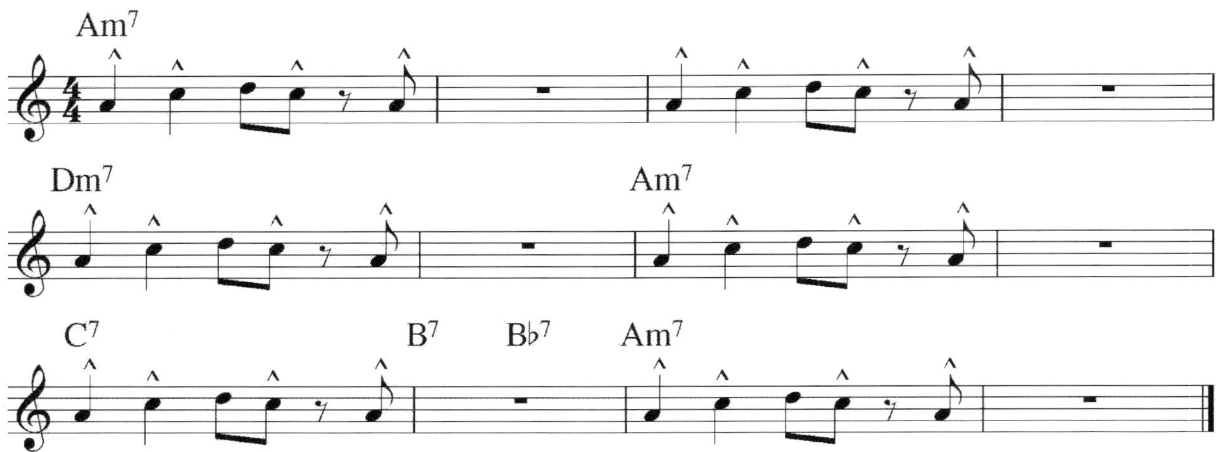

"Response" #1

"Longer Riff" #1

"Call" #2

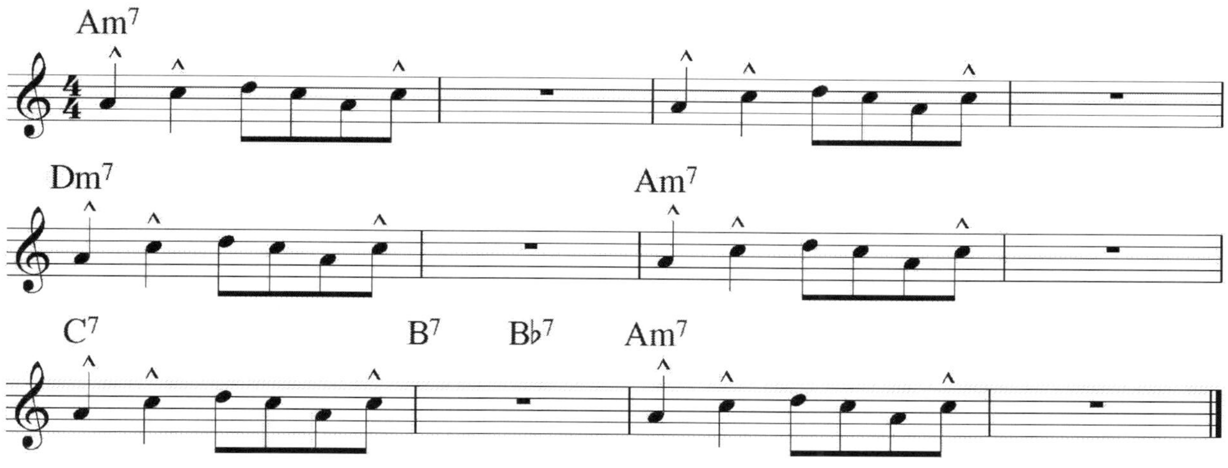

"Response" #2

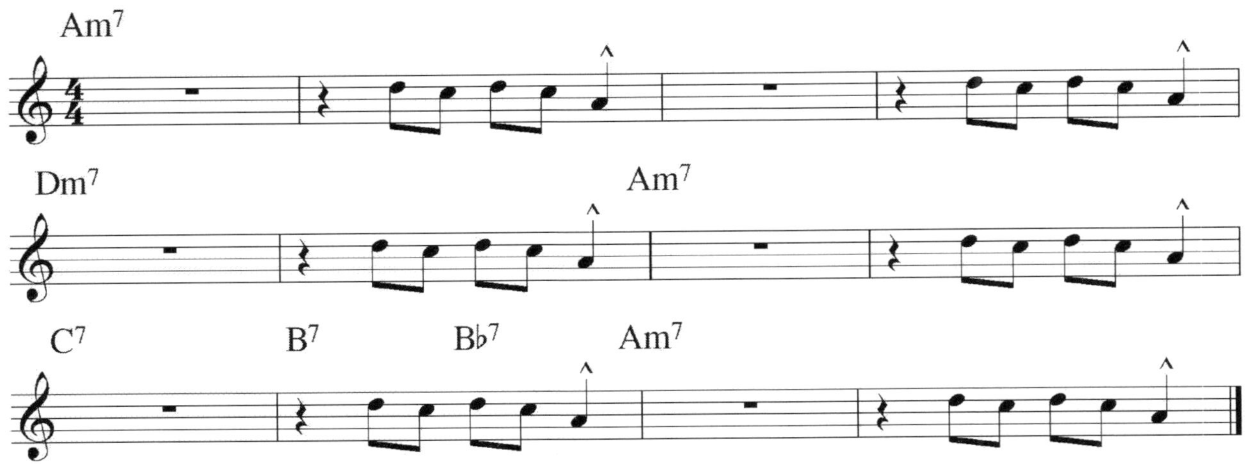

"Longer Riff" #2

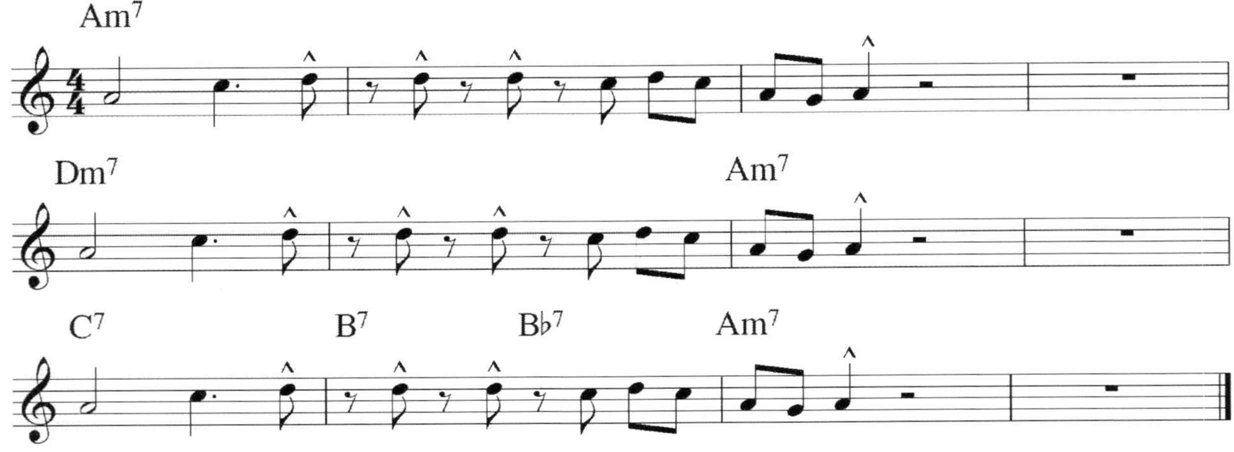

"Call" #3

"Response" #3

"Longer Riff" #3

"Call" #4

"Response" #4

"Longer Riff" #4

"Call" #5

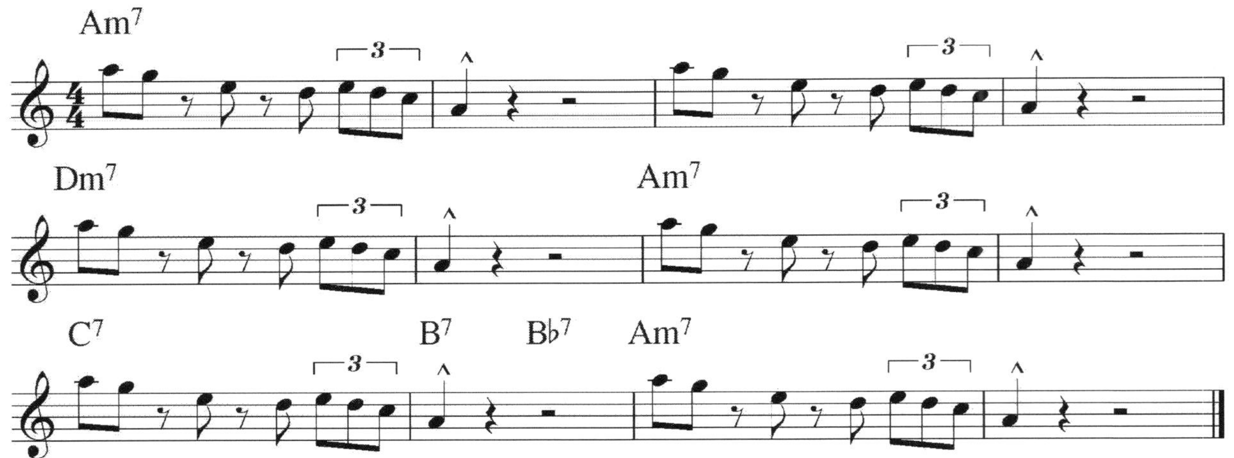

"Response" #5

"Longer Riff" #5

4 Sample Improvised Choruses using Minor Pentatonic Riffs

Chorus #1

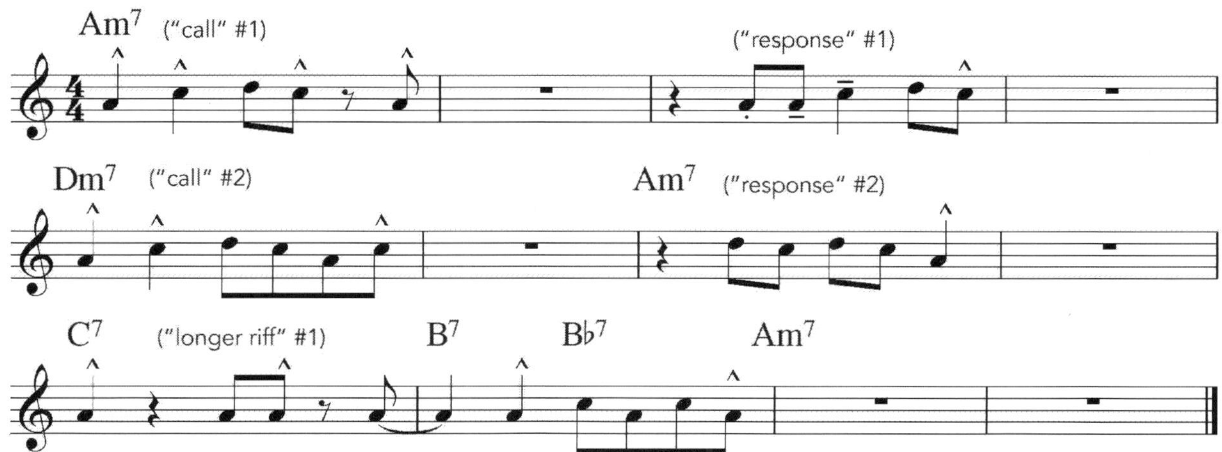

Chorus #2

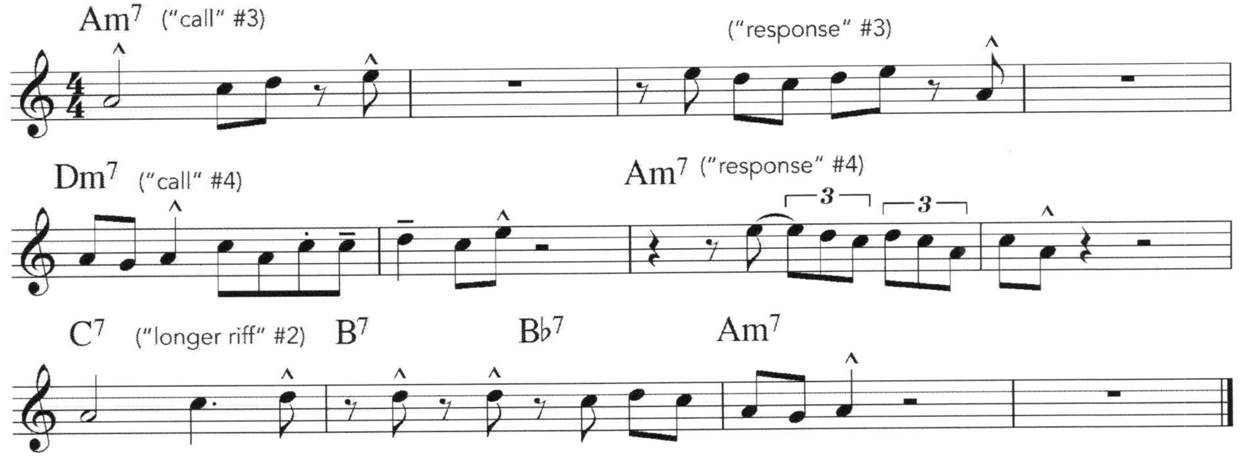

Chorus #3 — AAB phrases

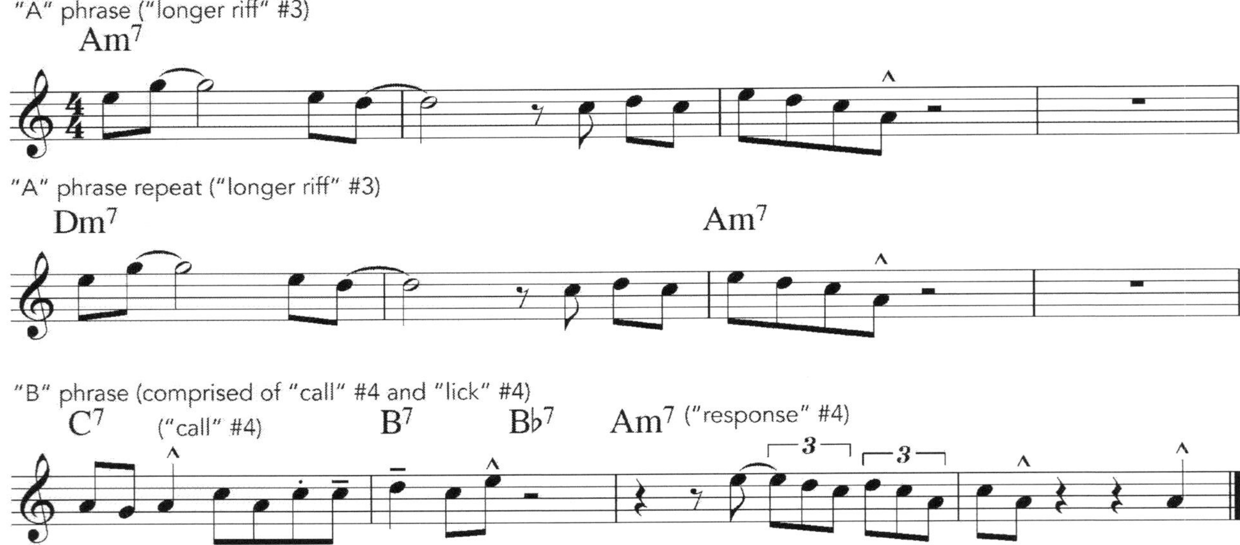

Chorus #4 — AAB phrases

Play an improvised solo using minor pentatonic riffs.

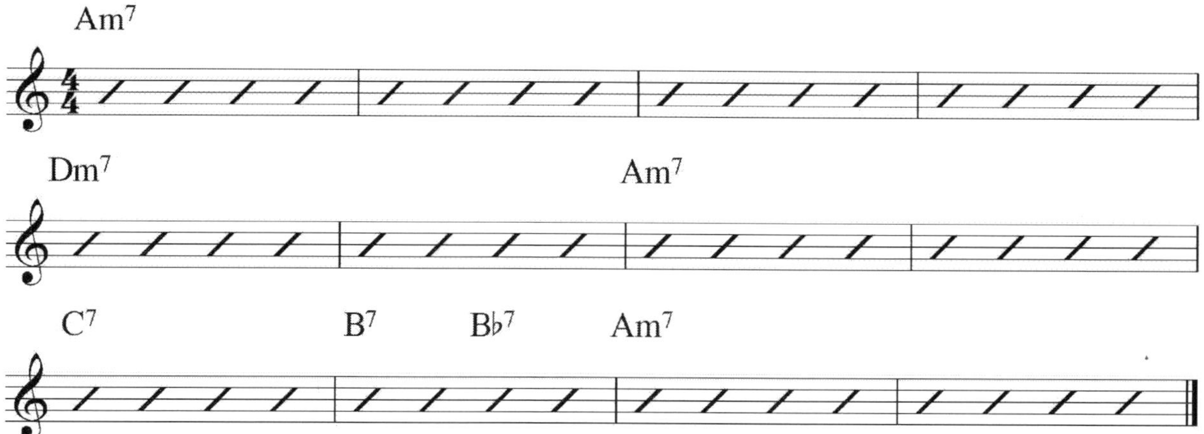

16-BAR BLUES IN F PRACTICE PROCEDURE

straight at 125 BPM

Roots

1a. Roots

Play an improvised solo using only the roots of the chord.

1b. Roots — sample improvised solo

1c. Roots — play an improvised solo using only roots

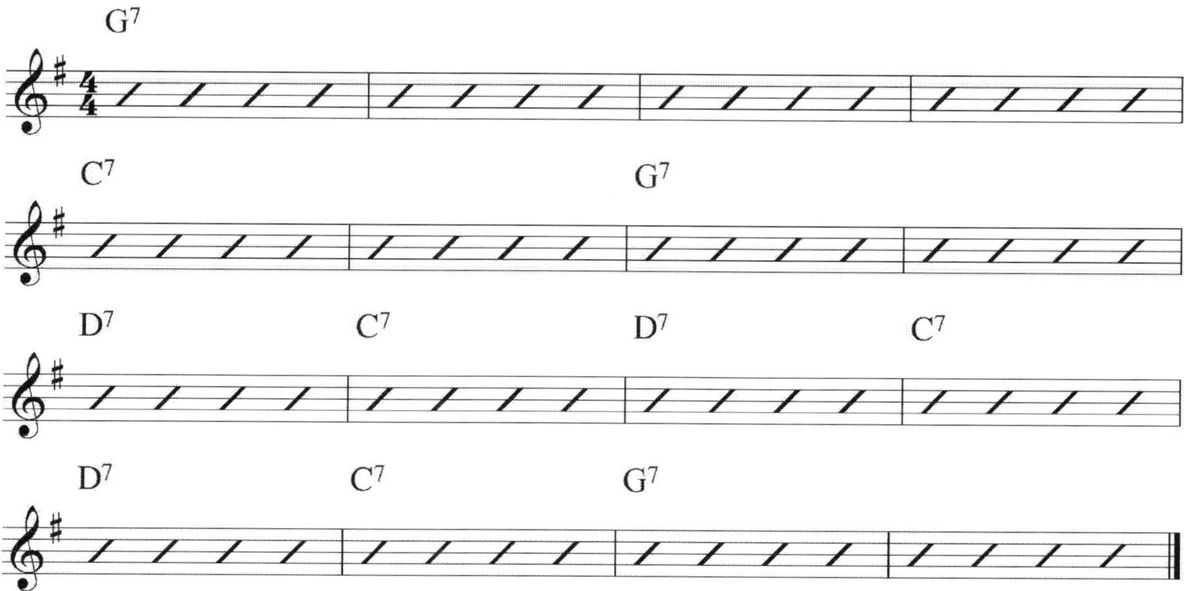

1, 2, 3's

2a. 1, 2, 3's — up up

2b. 1, 2, 3's — up down

2c. 1, 2, 3's — down up

2d. 1, 2, 3's — down down

Play an improvised solo using only 1, 2, 3's of each scale.

2e. 1, 2, 3's — sample improvised solo

2f. 1, 2, 3's — play an improvised solo using only 1, 2, 3's

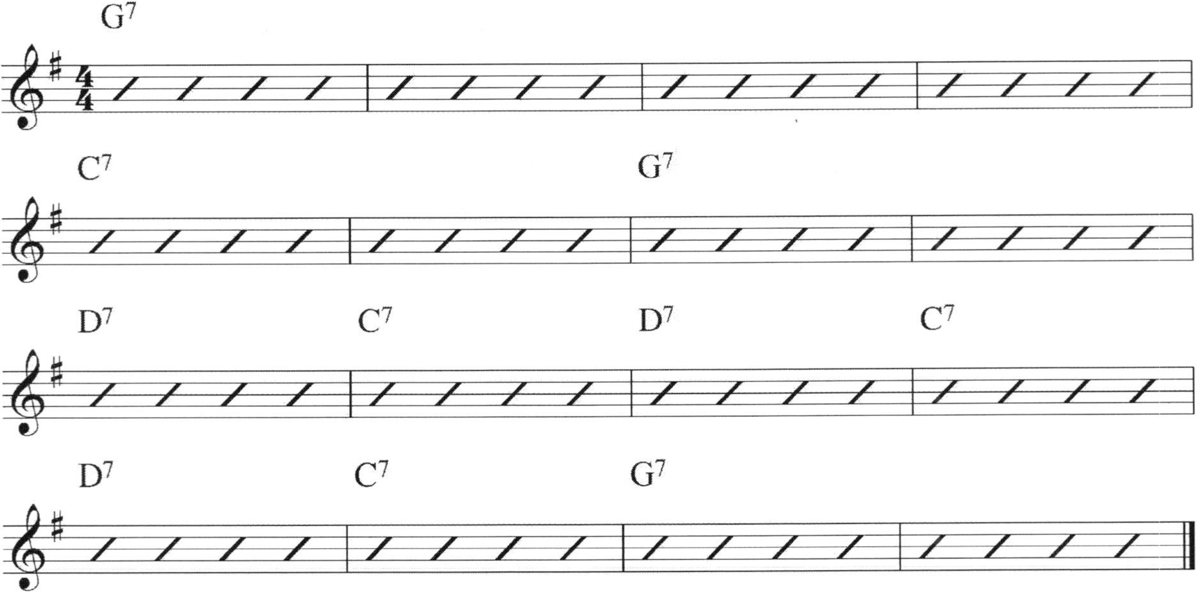

1, 2, 3, 4, 5's

3a. 1, 2, 3, 4, 5's — up up

3b. 1, 2, 3, 4, 5's — up down

3c. 1, 2, 3, 4, 5's — down up

3d. 1, 2, 3, 4, 5's — down down

Play an improvised solo using only 1, 2, 3, 4, 5's of each scale.

3e. 1, 2, 3, 4, 5's — sample improvised solo

3f. 1, 2, 3, 4, 5's — play an improvised solo using only 1, 2, 3, 4, 5's

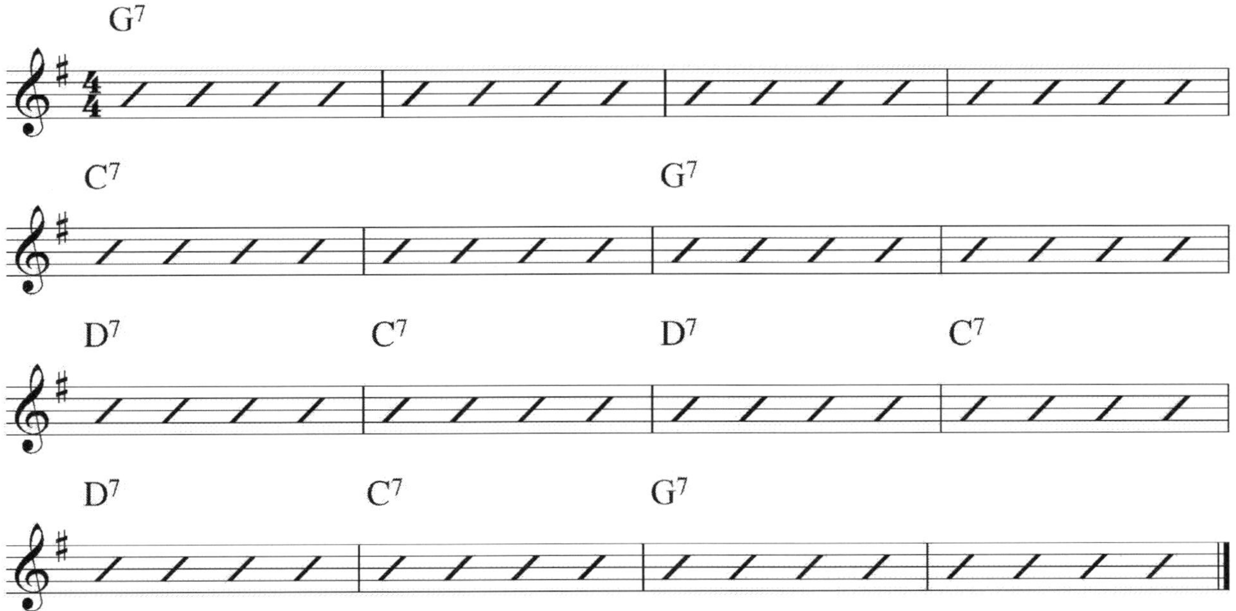

Full Scales

During perpetual motion exercises, stop to breathe, but keep your fingers, keys, and slides moving while breathing.

4a. Full scales — up up

4b. Full scales — up down

4c. Full scales — down up

4d. Full scales — down down

Play an improvised solo using any scale notes.

4e. Full scales — sample improvised solo

4f. Full scales — play an improvised solo using the full scale

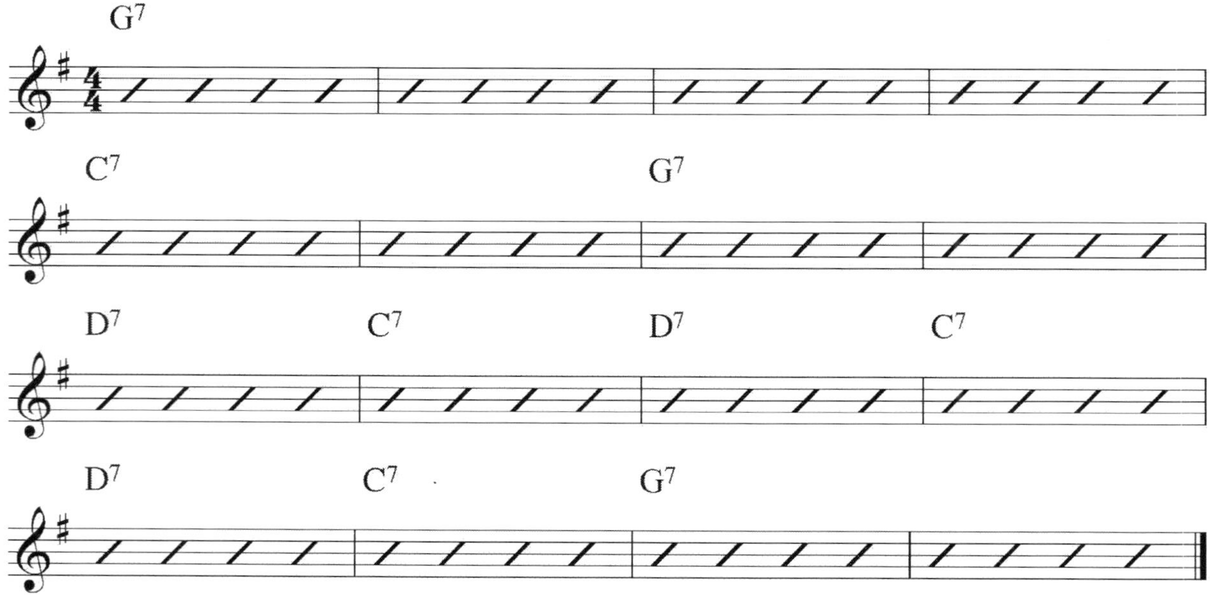

Chord Tone Workout

5a. 1, 3, 5, 7 — up up

5b. 1, 3, 5, 7 — up down

5c. 1, 3, 5, 7 — down up

5d. 1, 3, 5, 7 — down down

6a. 3, 5, 7, 1 — up up

6b. 3, 5, 7, 1 — up down

6c. 3, 5, 7, 1 — down up

6d. 3, 5, 7, 1 — down down

7a. 5, 7, 1, 3 — up up

7b. 5, 7, 1, 3 — up down

7c. 5, 7, 1, 3 — down up

7d. 5, 7, 1, 3 — down down

8a. 7, 1, 3, 5 — up up

8b. 7, 1, 3, 5 — up down

8c. 7, 1, 3, 5 — down up

8d. 7, 1, 3, 5 — down down

9. 16-Bar Blues Vocab

10. Running eighth-notes with chord tones on down beats

A to A (two octaves) — chromaticism used to connect when necessary

Minor Pentatonic Riffs

"Call" #1

"Response" #1

"Longer Riff" #1

"Call" #2

"Response" #2

"Longer Riff" #2

"Call" #3

"Response" #3

"Longer Riff" #3

"Call" #4

"Response" #4

"Longer Riff" #4

"Call" #5

"Response" #5

"Longer Riff" #5

4 Sample Improvised Choruses using Minor Pentatonic Riffs

Chorus #1

Chorus #2

Chorus #3 — AAB phrases

Chorus #4 — AAB phrases

Play an improvised solo using minor pentatonic riffs.

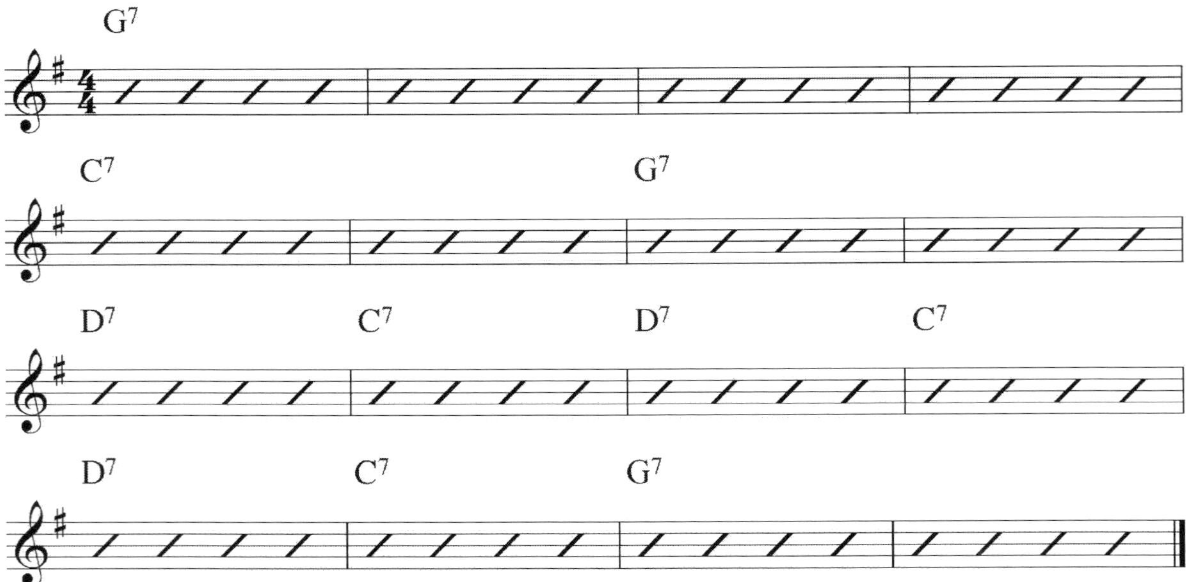

SAMPLE PIANO VOICINGS

Swing @ 120 bpm

B♭7 Add rhythmic variety | E♭7 | B♭7 | B♭7

E♭7 | E♭7 | B♭7 | G7

Cm7 | F7 | B♭7 | F7

Swing @ 105 bpm

Voicings option #1

Straight @ 135 bpm

Gm7 Add rhythmic variety Gm7 Gm7 Gm7

Cm7 Cm7 Gm7 Gm7

B♭7 A7 A♭7 Gm7 Gm7

Straight @ 125 bpm

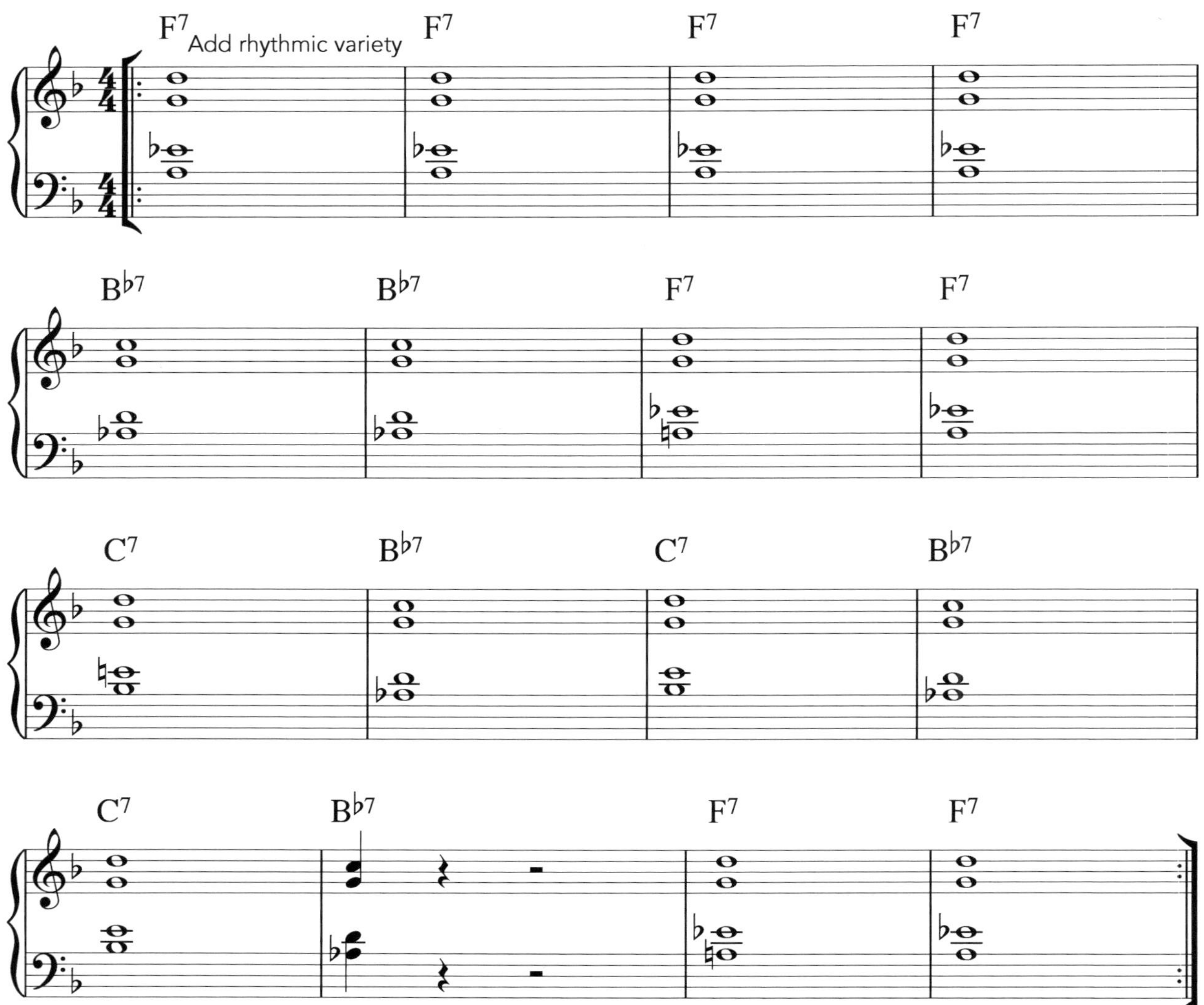

About the Author

Doug Stone's career has involved work as a touring musician, primarily with jazz trumpet legend Maynard Ferguson and his band, the Big Bop Nouveau, as well as with the "world-jazz" group Panoramic, and with a number of ensembles from Chicago, Illinois. His time on the road has taken him to virtually every corner of the United States as well as Asia, Europe, the Caribbean, and Canada. As a member of groups at Northern Illinois University, Stone had the opportunity to perform with Frank Foster, Benny Golson, Frank Wess, Jimmy Heath, Rufus Reid, Larry Ridley, and Carl Allen. As a member of the Birch Creek Academy Band he has performed with jazz luminaries Dennis Mackrel, Harold Jones, Derrick Gardner, Tanya Darby, Reggie Thomas, and Clay Jenkins. He spent six years working full-time as a freelance saxophonist and woodwind player, teacher, composer, and arranger in the rich musical environment of Chicago.

Mr. Stone can be heard on recordings from the Sam Craine Quartet, the Dave Hoffman Sextet, the NIU Jazz Ensemble and Jazztet, the Jazz Arranging Syndicate, Birch Creek Academy Big Band, the Ed Breazeale Group, the Ji Young Lee Quartet, the Stuart Mindeman Group, the Ian Torres Big Band, the John Burnett Orchestra, Panoramic, Quintopus, the Rick Holland Little Big Band, the Rich Thompson Quartet and Trio, the Westview Project, the John Nyerges Quintet, the Bob DiBaudo ensemble, the Eric Schmitz Sextet, and the Tom Marko ensemble. Stone has four recordings to his credit as a co-bandleader: Doug Stone/Josiah Williams "The Early Riser", Stone/Ziemba Duo "In the Zone", Nick Fryer/Doug Stone "Quartet", and The Stone/Bratt Big Band "SBBB".

Stone is also a published arranger and composer (Kendor Music). His compositions and arrangements have been performed by professional, university, and high school level jazz ensembles throughout the United States.

In 2009 Mr. Stone moved to Rochester, New York to pursue a double master's degree in jazz performance and music education at the Eastman School of Music. He has performed in Rochester with the Dave Rivello Ensemble, the Westview Project, the Gap Mangione Big Band, Quintopus, the John Nyerges Duo and Quartet, Jeff Campbell, Rich Thompson, and other talented local jazz artists. While in western New York, Stone has worked with several noteworthy musicians including George Caldwell, Bobby Militello, Harold Danko, Gene Bertoncini, Bill Dobbins, Mark Ferber, Ike Sturm, Charles Pillow, Allen Vizzutti, and the Mambo Kings.

Since 2009 Mr. Stone has taught private lessons, ensembles, and classes at the Eastman Community Music School (ECMS). He has also served as chair of the ECMS jazz department and has directed the prestigious Eastman Youth Jazz Orchestra.

In 2012 Mr. Stone accepted a position as the director of jazz ensembles at the Rochester School of the Arts (SOTA) in Rochester, New York. He taught several ensembles, classes, and lessons at SOTA.

In the summers Mr. Stone teaches at the Eastman Summer Jazz Studies Program, the Tri-Tone Jazz Camp, has previously served as co-director of the Eastman at Keuka College Jazz Camp, and served as assistant to the director at the Birch Creek Jazz Camp.

Mr. Stone has held teaching positions at The State University of New York at Brockport, the Northern Illinois University Community School of the Arts in DeKalb, IL, and he worked as private saxophone, jazz, and small group instructor at St. Charles North High School in St. Charles, IL.

Mr. Stone is now serving as the Associate Professor of Jazz Studies at Louisiana State University where he conducts the Jazz Ensemble. Mr. Stone is the past president of the Louisiana Association for Jazz Educators and the LMEA Jazz Division Chairperson.

Made in the USA
Columbia, SC
02 July 2025